WILLIAM BLAKE

Selected
Poems

WILLIAM BLAKE

Selected Poems

GRAMERCY BOOKS
New York • Avenel

This 1995 edition is published by Gramercy Books,
a division of Random House Value Publishing, Inc.,
40 Engelhard Avenue, Avenel, New Jersey 07001.

Gramercy Books and colophon are trademarks of
Random House Value Publishing, Inc.

Random House
New York • Toronto • London • Sydney • Auckland
http://www.randomhouse.com/

Printed and bound in the United States of America

Library of Congress Cataloging-in-Publication Data
Blake, William 1757-1827
[Poems. Selections]
Selected poems / William Blake.
p.   cm.
ISBN 0-517-12367-3
I. Title.
PR4142   1995
821'.7—dc20   94-23674   CIP

8   7   6   5   4   3   2

CONTENTS

Songs of Innocence

Songs of Experience

From the Rossetti Manuscript

The Pickering Manuscript

Miscellaneous Works

The Book of Thel

Visions of the Daughters of Albion

The Marriage of Heaven and Hell

America: A Prophecy

Europe: A Prophecy

INTRODUCTION

From his early years, William Blake's distinctive imagination marked him as uncommon. The second of five children of a haberdasher, he was born in Carnaby Market, London, on November 28, 1757. At the age of four he began to have visions of God and of angels appearing to him on the street. He was taught to read and write at home and was apprenticed for seven years to James Basire, an engraver. Then, in 1779, Blake received his only formal education, attending the Royal Academy of Arts for a very short period. Iconoclastic and rebellious, he was, it seemed, ill-suited to the constraints of the classroom.

Though considered an ingenious artist by many of his peers, Blake was temperamentally difficult and intractable. All through his career he refused to compromise his personal vision, even when commissioned to illustrate other people's books—which was the main source of income for an engraver. This put him at a definite disadvantage in London, where the competition for work was cutthroat.

In 1782, Blake married Catherine Boucher, the daughter of a market-gardener. Though the marriage was childless, theirs was a lasting union that weathered all the difficult times of hardship and poverty. Catherine was illiterate when she married—she signed the marriage certificate with an "X"—but Blake taught her to read and write, and to help him with his engraving and printing work when, in 1784, he opened a printshop. The business, however, failed after only a year.

Throughout most of his life, Blake eked out a meager living from the sporadic jobs he was able to obtain and through the consistent and charitable patronage of several benefactors. His only attempt at widespread recognition, a one-man show of sixteen paintings in 1809, was a complete failure. But in 1818 he met

John Linnell, who became one of his chief supporters and helped make the last years of his life relatively stable and untroubled. When Blake died on August 12, 1827, at the age of sixty-nine, he was surrounded by a small, loyal group of young avant-garde artists who considered him a master.

Recognition of Blake as a poet, however, did not come until years after his death. In his lifetime, he was isolated from the mainstream literary and art circles. Contemporaries who were aware of his poetry had varied opinions. Charles Lamb and Samuel Taylor Coleridge, for example, thought highly of parts of Blake's *Songs of Innocence and of Experience*, while William Wordsworth wrote him off as insane. By the end of the nineteenth century, however, Blake's literary reputation was on the rise. He was being championed by such eminent poets as William Butler Yeats, who comprehended the psychological and symbolic richness of Blake's poetry, which had been overlooked or misunderstood by earlier generations. T. S. Eliot, one of the twentieth century's most celebrated poets and critics, wrote that Blake's works have "the peculiarity of all great poetry: something which is . . . profound."

In contrast to most other poets, Blake was unusual because he was also an accomplished painter and engraver who conceived and executed most of his major works as illustrated books. He printed and published them himself using his own unique method of engraving. Covering copper plate with acid-proof wax, he engraved away the wax to form a design that integrated both the text and the illustrations, then applied acid so that the design was left in relief. Blake hand-colored each page and bound them, a laboriously slow process that generated only limited quantities of his work. Today, only twenty-seven copies of the original edition of *Songs of Innocence and of Experience* have survived.

Although he is now categorized as part of the Romantic Movement, Blake was not a member of the group of poets led by Wordsworth and Coleridge. He was of a different social class and he was older—he was forty when their *Lyrical Ballads*, the ground-breaking manifesto of the Romantic Movement, was published. While Blake did have several things in common with them, like support for the French Revolution and a radical anti-establishment viewpoint, he differed in his conception and moti-vation for writing poetry. At the beginning of his artistic career he made a conscious decision to follow his "Divine Vision," though it meant a life of isolation and poverty. Blake claimed that "all he knew was in the Bible" and that "the Old & New Testaments are the Great Code of Art." He was much closer in spirit and inspiration to John Milton and Dante than to the other English Romantics.

Blake taught himself Greek and Hebrew well enough to read the Bible in the original languages, but, characteristically, he had an idiosyncratic and personal interpretation of Christianity. He was influenced in part by the beliefs of Emanuel Swedenborg, the scientist, mystic, and leader of one of the great religious movements of the eighteenth century. Although Blake was a member of London's Swedenborgian Church of New Jerusalem only briefly before he became disillusioned with it, the beliefs of this church had a lasting effect upon his imagina-tion. Reflected in Blake's works is Swedenborg's emphasis on the idea of a Christianity that is based, not on the separate nature of the divine and human, but on the unity of God and Man in Christ. Also evident is Swedenborg's apocalyptic per-spective and his belief in the "correspondence" between physi-cal and spiritual worlds. But as the works collected in this vol-ume illustrate, Blake was not one to be constrained by church dogma, and his spiritual and creative conceptions evolved beyond his influences.

Poetical Sketches is a collection of Blake's earliest poems, most of them written before 1778, when he was twenty-one, but not published until 1783. Unlike his later works, it is not illustrated. Poems like "To the Evening Star" clearly show the influence of the Elizabethans and such early seventeenth-century poets as Milton. The rest of the works in this book were written between 1788 and 1795, his most creative period.

Songs of Innocence, the first of Blake's illustrated books, was published individually in 1789, and then combined with *Songs of Experience* in 1794 with the subtitle: "Showing the two contrary states of the human soul." *Songs of Innocence and of Experience* is considered one of the masterpieces of English literature and includes some of his most popular poems, including "The Lamb," "The Chimney Sweeper," and "The Tyger." Blake's principal inspiration was the illuminated manuscripts of the Middle Ages, but instead of biblical stories, he was presenting his own personal and original vision.

Also included are selections from Blake's notebooks—the "Rossetti Manuscript" and the "Pickering Manuscript"—which include poetic fragments and alternative versions of some of his poems.

Blake was the untiring rebel who fought against all constrictions—religious, social, sexual, and literary—that he believed were impediments to true spiritual fulfillment. In *The Marriage of Heaven and Hell,* published in 1790, he wickedly satirizes all known ideas of religious orthodoxy. It is a truly funny work in which he reverses the traditional ideas of good and evil: the devil and his associates are depicted as energetic and creative, while the angels are bland, timid, and lethargic.

The other longer works included here—*The Book of Thel* (1789), *Visions of the Daughters of Albion* (1793), *America: A Prophecy* (1793), and *Europe: A Prophecy* (1794)—are his so-called minor prophecies. In these works he began to create his own mythology, which he continued to expand upon in his later works, the major prophetic books: *The Four Zoas, Milton,* and *Jerusalem.* He wrote, "I must Create a System or be enslaved by another Man's." Through recurring characters, which he called the "Giant Forms"—Orc, the passionate spirit of revolution, for example, and Los, who represents visionary imagination—Blake reinterprets the spiritual history of the human race from the fall of man to the French Revolution. For Blake, the Revolution destroyed the old, decaying order and was an event of apocalyptic significance that presaged the redemption of humanity on the verge of a new millennium.

CHRISTOPHER MOORE

New York
1995

From
Poetical
Sketches

TO SPRING

O thou, with dewy locks, who lookest down
Thro' the clear windows of the morning, turn
Thine angel eyes upon our western isle,
Which in full choir hails thy approach, O Spring!

The hills tell each other, and the list'ning
Valleys hear; all our longing eyes are turned
Up to thy bright pavillions: issue forth,
And let thy holy feet visit our clime.

Come o'er the eastern hills, and let our winds
Kiss thy perfumed garments; let us taste
Thy morn and evening breath; scatter thy pearls
Upon our lovesick land that mourns for thee.

O deck her forth with thy fair fingers; pour
Thy soft kisses on her bosom; and put
Thy golden crown upon her languish'd head,
Whose modest tresses were bound up for thee!

TO SUMMER

O thou, who passest thro' our valleys in
Thy strength, curb thy fierce steeds, allay the heat
That flames from their large nostrils! thou, O Summer,
Oft pitched'st here thy golden tent, and oft
Beneath our oaks hast slept, while we beheld
With joy, thy ruddy limbs and flourishing hair.

Beneath our thickest shades we oft have heard
Thy voice, when noon upon his fervid ear
Rode o'er the deep of heaven; beside our springs
Sit down, and in our mossy valleys, on
Some bank beside a river clear, throw thy
Silk draperies off, and rush into the stream:
Our valleys love the Summer in his pride.

Our bards are fam'd who strike the silver wire:
Our youth are bolder than the southern swains:
Our maidens fairer in the sprightly dance:
We lack not songs, nor instruments of joy,
Nor echoes sweet, nor waters clear as heaven,
Nor laurel wreaths against the sultry heat.

TO AUTUMN

O Autumn, laden with fruit, and stained
With the blood of the grape, pass not, but sit
Beneath my shady roof; there thou may'st rest,
And tune thy jolly voice to my fresh pipe;
And all the daughters of the year shall dance!
Sing now the lusty song of fruits and flowers.

"The narrow bud opens her beauties to
The sun, and love runs in her thrilling veins;
Blossoms hang round the brows of morning, and
Flourish down the bright cheek of modest eve,
Till clust'ring Summer breaks forth into singing,
And feather'd clouds strew flowers round her head.

"The spirits of the air live on the smells
Of fruit; and joy, with pinions light, roves round
The gardens, or sits singing in the trees."
Thus sang the jolly Autumn as he sat,
Then rose, girded himself, and o'er the bleak
Hills fled from our sight; but left his golden load.

TO WINTER

O Winter! bar thine adamantine doors:
The north is thine; there hast thou built thy dark
Deep-founded habitation. Shake not thy roofs,
Nor bend thy pillars with thine iron car.

He hears me not, but o'er the yawning deep
Rides heavy; his storms are unchain'd; sheathed
In ribbed steel, I dare not lift mine eyes;
For he hath rear'd his scepter o'er the world.

Lo! now the direful monster, whose skin clings
To his strong bones, strides o'er the groaning rocks:
He withers all in silence, and his hand
Unclothes the earth, and freezes up frail life.

He takes his seat upon the cliffs, the mariner
Cries in vain. Poor little wretch! that deal'st
With storms; till heaven smiles, and the monster
Is driv'n yelling to his caves beneath mount Hecla.

TO THE EVENING STAR

Thou fair-hair'd angel of the evening,
Now, whilst the sun rests on the mountains, light
Thy bright torch of love; thy radiant crown
Put on, and smile upon our evening bed!
Smile on our loves; and, while thou drawest the
Blue curtains of the sky, scatter thy silver dew
On every flower that shuts its sweet eyes
In timely sleep. Let thy west wind sleep on
The lake; speak silence with thy glimmering eyes,
And wash the dusk with silver. Soon, full soon,
Dost thou withdraw, then the wolf rages wide,
And the lion glares thro' the dun forest:
The fleeces of our flocks are cover'd with
Thy sacred dew: protect them with thine influence.

TO MORNING

O holy virgin! clad in purest white,
Unlock heav'n's golden gates, and issue forth;
Awake the dawn that sleeps in heaven; let light
Rise from the chambers of the east, and bring
The honied dew that cometh on waking day.
O radiant morning, salute the sun,
Rous'd like a huntsman to the chase; and, with
Thy buskin'd feet, appear upon our hills.

FAIR ELENOR

The bell struck one, and shook the silent tower;
The graves give up their dead: fair Elenor
Walk'd by the castle gate, and looked in.
A hollow groan ran thro' the dreary vaults.

She shriek'd aloud, and sunk upon the steps
On the cold stone her pale cheek. Sickly smells
Of death, issue as from a sepulcher,
And all is silent but the sighing vaults.

Chill death withdraws his hand, and she revives;
Amaz'd, she finds herself upon her feet,
And, like a ghost, thro' narrow passages
Walking, feeling the cold walls with her hands.

Fancy returns, and now she thinks of bones,
And grinning skulls, and corruptible death,
Wrapp'd in his shroud; and now, fancies she hears
Deep sighs, and sees pale sickly ghosts gliding.

At length, no fancy, but reality
Distracts her. A rushing sound, and the feet
Of one that fled, approaches—Ellen stood,
Like a dumb statue, froze to stone with fear.

The wretch approaches, crying, "The deed is done;
Take this, and send it by whom thou wilt send;
It is my life—send it to Elenor—
He's dead, and howling after me for blood!

"Take this," he cried; and thrust into her arms
A wet napkin, wrapp'd about; then rush'd

Past, howling: she receiv'd into her arms
Pale death, and follow'd on the wings of fear.

They pass'd swift thro' the outer gate; the wretch,
Howling, leap'd o'er the wall into the moat,
Stifling in mud. Fair Ellen pass'd the bridge,
And heard a gloomy voice cry, "Is it done?"

As the deer wounded Ellen flew over
The pathless plain; as the arrows that fly
By night; destruction flies, and strikes in darkness,
She fled from fear, till at her house arriv'd.

Her maids await her; on her bed she falls,
That bed of joy, where erst her lord hath press'd:
"Ah, woman's fear!" she cried; "Ah, cursed duke!
Ah, my dear lord! ah, wretched Elenor!

"My lord was like a flower upon the brows
Of lusty May! Ah, life as frail as flower!
O ghastly death! withdraw thy cruel hand,
Seek'st thou that flow'r to deck thy horrid temples?

"My lord was like a star, in highest heav'n
Drawn down to earth by spells and wickedness:
My lord was like the opening eyes of day,
When western winds creep softly o'er the flowers:

"But he is darken'd; like the summer's noon,
Clouded; fall'n like the stately tree, cut down;
The breath of heaven dwelt among his leaves.
O Elenor, weak woman, fill'd with woe!"

Thus having spoke, she raised up her head,
And saw the bloody napkin by her side,

Which in her arms she brought; and now, tenfold
More terrified, saw it unfold itself.

Her eyes were fix'd; the bloody cloth unfolds,
Disclosing to her sight the murder'd head
Of her dear lord, all ghastly pale, clotted
With gory blood; it groan'd, and thus it spake:

"O Elenor, behold thy husband's head,
Who, sleeping on the stones of yonder tower,
Was 'reft of life by the accursed duke!
A hired villain turn'd my sleep to death!

"O Elenor, beware the cursed duke,
O give not him thy hand, now I am dead;
He seeks thy love; who, coward, in the night,
Hired a villain to bereave my life."

She sat with dead cold limbs, stiffen'd to stone;
She took the gory head up in her arms;
She kiss'd the pale lips; she had no tears to shed;
She hugg'd it to her breast, and groan'd her last.

SONG

How sweet I roam'd from field to field,
    And tasted all the summer's pride,
'Till I the prince of love beheld,
    Who in the sunny beams did glide!

He show'd me lilies for my hair,
And blushing roses for my brow;
He led me through his gardens fair,
    Where all his golden pleasures grow.

With sweet May dews my wings were wet,
    And Phoebus fir'd my vocal rage;
He caught me in his silken net,
    And shut me in his golden cage.

He loves to sit and hear me sing,
    Then, laughing, sports and plays with me;
Then stretches out my golden wing,
    And mocks my loss of liberty.

SONG

My silks and fine array,
　My smiles and languish'd air,
By love are driv'n away;
　And mournful lean Despair
Brings me yew to deck my grave:
Such end true lovers have.

His face is fair as heav'n,
　When springing buds unfold;
O why to him was't giv'n,
　Whose heart is wintry cold?
His breast is love's all worship'd tomb,
Where all love's pilgrims come.

Bring me an axe and spade,
　Bring me a winding sheet;
When I my grave have made,
　Let winds and tempests beat:
Then down I'll lie, as cold as clay.
True love doth pass away!

SONG

Love and harmony combine,
And around our souls entwine,
While thy branches mix with mine,
And our roots together join.

Joys upon our branches sit,
Chirping loud, and singing sweet;
Like gentle streams beneath our feet
Innocence and virtue meet.

Thou the golden fruit dost bear,
I am clad in flowers fair;
Thy sweet boughs perfume the air,
And the turtle buildeth there.

There she sits and feeds her young,
Sweet I hear her mournful song;
And thy lovely leaves among,
There is love: I hear his tongue.

There his charming nest doth lay,
There he sleeps the night away;
There he sports along the day,
And doth among our branches play.

SONG

I love the jocund dance,
   The softly-breathing song,
Where innocent eyes do glance,
   And where lisps the maiden's tongue.

I love the laughing vale,
   I love the echoing hill,
Where mirth does never fail,
   And the jolly swain laughs his fill.

I love the pleasant cot,
   I love the innocent bow'r.
Where white and brown is our lot,
   Or fruit in the midday hour.

I love the oaken seat,
   Beneath the oaken tree,
Where all the old villagers meet,
   And laugh our sports to see.

I love our neighbors all,
   But, Kitty, I better love thee;
And love them I ever shall;
   But thou art all to me.

SONG

Memory, hither come,
   And tune your merry notes;
And, while upon the wind,
   Your music floats,
I'll pore upon the stream,
Where sighing lovers dream,
And fish for fancies as they pass
Within the watery glass.

I'll drink of the clear stream,
   And hear the linnet's song;
And there I'll lie and dream
   The day along:
And, when night comes, I'll go
To places fit for woe;
Walking along the darken'd valley,
   With silent Melancholy.

MAD SONG

The wild winds weep,
   And the night is a-cold;
Come hither, Sleep,
   And my griefs enfold:
But lo! the morning peeps
   Over the eastern steeps,
And the rustling birds of dawn
The earth do scorn.

Lo! to the vault
   Of paved heaven,
With sorrow fraught
   My notes are driven:
They strike the ear of night,
   Make weep the eyes of day;
They make mad the roaring winds,
   And with tempests play.

Like a fiend in a cloud
   With howling woe,
After night I do crowd,
   And with night will go;
I turn my back to the east,
From whence comforts have increas'd;
For light doth seize my brain
With frantic pain.

SONG

Fresh from the dewy hill, the merry year
Smiles on my head, and mounts his flaming car;
Round my young brows the laurel wreathes a shade,
And rising glories beam around my head.

My feet are wing'd, while o'er the dewy lawn,
I meet my maiden, risen like the morn:
Oh bless those holy feet, like angels' feet;
Oh bless those limbs, beaming with heav'nly light!

Like as an angel glitt'ring in the sky,
In times of innocence, and holy joy;
The joyful shepherd stops his grateful song,
To hear the music of an angel's tongue.

So when she speaks, the voice of Heaven I hear;
So when we walk, nothing impure comes near;
Each field seems Eden, and each calm retreat;
Each village seems the haunt of holy feet.

But that sweet village where my black-ey'd maid,
Closes her eyes in sleep beneath night's shade:
Whene'er I enter, more than mortal fire
Burns in my soul, and does my song inspire.

SONG

When early morn walks forth in sober gray;
Then to my black-ey'd maid I haste away,
When evening sits beneath her dusky bow'r,
And gently sighs away the silent hour;
The village bell alarms, away I go;
And the vale darkens at my pensive woe.

To that sweet village, where my black-ey'd maid
Doth drop a tear beneath the silent shade,
I turn my eyes; and, pensive as I go,
Curse my black stars, and bless my pleasing woe.

Oft when the summer sleeps among the trees,
Whisp'ring faint murmurs to the scanty breeze,
I walk the village round; if at her side
A youth doth walk in stolen joy and pride,
I curse my stars in bitter grief and woe,
That made my love so high, and me so low.

O should she e'er prove false, his limbs I'd tear,
And throw all pity on the burning air;
I'd curse bright fortune for my mixed lot,
And then I'd die in peace, and be forgot.

TO THE MUSES

Whether on Ida's shady brow,
   Or in the chambers of the East,
The chambers of the sun, that now
   From antient melody have ceas'd;

Whether in Heav'n ye wander fair,
   Or the green corners of the earth,
Or the blue regions of the air,
   Where the melodious winds have birth;

Whether on crystal rocks ye rove,
   Beneath the bosom of the sea
Wand'ring in many a coral grove,
   Fair Nine, forsaking Poetry!

How have you left the antient love
   That bards of old enjoy'd in you!
The languid strings do scarcely move!
   The sound is forc'd, the notes are few!

GWIN, KING OF NORWAY

Come, Kings, and listen to my song,
  When Gwin, the son of Nore,
Over the nations of the North
  His cruel scepter bore:

The Nobles of the land did feed
  Upon the hungry Poor;
They tear the poor man's lamb, and drive
  The needy from their door!

The land is desolate; our wives
  And children cry for bread;
Arise, and pull the tyrant down;
  Let Gwin be humbled.

Gordred the giant rous'd himself
  From sleeping in his cave;
He shook the hills, and in the clouds
  The troubl'd banners wave.

Beneath them roll'd, like tempests black,
  The num'rous sons of blood;
Like lions' whelps, roaring abroad,
  Seeking their nightly food.

Down Bleron's hills they dreadful rush,
  Their cry ascends the clouds;
The trampling horse, and clanging arms
  Like rushing mighty floods!

Their wives and children, weeping loud,
  Follow in wild array,

Howling like ghosts, furious as wolves
    In the bleak wintry day.

"Pull down the tyrant to the dust,
    Let Gwin be humbled,"
They cry; "and let ten thousand lives
    Pay for the tyrant's head."

From tow'r to tow'r the watchmen cry,
    "O Gwin, the son of Nore,
Arouse thyself! the nations black,
    Like clouds, come rolling o'er!"

Gwin rear'd his shield, his palace shakes,
    His chiefs come rushing round;
Each, like an awful thundercloud,
    With voice of solemn sound.

Like reared stones around a grave
    They stand around the King;
Then suddenly each seiz'd his spear,
    And clashing steel does ring.

The husbandman does leave his plow,
    To wade thro' fields of gore;
The merchant binds his brows in steel,
    And leaves the trading shore:

The shepherd leaves his mellow pipe,
    And sounds the trumpet shrill;
The workman throws his hammer down
    To heave the bloody bill.

Like the tall ghost of Barraton,
    Who sports in stormy sky,
Gwin leads his host as black as night,
    When pestilence does fly.

With horses and with chariots—
    And all his spearmen bold,
March to the sound of mournful song,
    Like clouds around him roll'd.

Gwin lifts his hand—the nations halt;
    "Prepare for war," he cries—
Gordred appears!—his frowning brow
    Troubles our northern skies.

The armies stand, like balances
    Held in th' Almighty's hand—
"Gwin, thou hast fill'd thy measure up,
    Thou'rt swept from out the land."

And now the raging armies rush'd,
    Like warring mighty seas;
The Heav'ns are shook with roaring war,
    The dust ascends the skies!

Earth smokes with blood, and groans, and shakes,
    To drink her childrens' gore,
A sea of blood; nor can the eye
    See to the trembling shore!

And on the verge of this wild sea
    Famine and death doth cry;
The cries of women and of babes
    Over the field doth fly.

The King is seen raging afar;
    With all his men of might;
Like blazing comets, scattering death
    Thro' the red fev'rous night.

Beneath his arm like sheep they die,
    And groan upon the plain;
The battle faints, and bloody men
    Fight upon hills of slain.

Now death is sick, and riven men
    Labor and toil for life;
Steed rolls on steed, and shield on shield,
    Sunk in this sea of strife!

The god of war is drunk with blood,
    The earth doth faint and fail;
The stench of blood makes sick the heav'ns;
    Ghosts glut the throat of hell!

O what have Kings to answer for,
    Before that awful throne!
When thousand deaths for vengeance cry,
    And ghosts accusing groan!

Like blazing comets in the sky,
    That shake the stars of light,
Which drop like fruit unto the earth,
    Thro' the fierce burning night;

Like these did Gwin and Gordred meet,
    And the first blow decides;
Down from the brow unto the breast
    Gordred his head divides!

Gwin fell; the Sons of Norway fled,
    All that remain'd alive;
The rest did fill the vale of death,
    For them the eagles strive.

The river Dorman roll'd their blood
    Into the northern sea;
Who mourn'd his sons, and overwhelm'd
    The pleasant south country.

PROLOGUE,
INTENDED FOR A DRAMATIC PIECE OF KING EDWARD THE FOURTH

O for a voice like thunder, and a tongue
To drown the throat of war!—When the senses
Are shaken, and the soul is driven to madness,
Who can stand? When the souls of the oppressed
Fight in the troubled air that rages, who can stand?
When the whirlwind of fury comes from the
Throne of God, when the frowns of his countenance
Drive the nations together, who can stand?
When Sin claps his broad wings over the battle,
And sails rejoicing in the flood of Death;
When souls are torn to everlasting fire,
And fiends of Hell rejoice upon the slain,
O who can stand? O who hath caused this?
O who can answer at the throne of God?
The Kings and Nobles of the Land have done it!
Hear it not, Heaven, thy Ministers have done it!

A WAR SONG
TO ENGLISHMEN

Prepare, prepare, the iron helm of war,
Bring forth the lots, cast in the spacious orb;
Th' Angel of Fate turns them with mighty hands,
And casts them out upon the darken'd earth!
        Prepare, prepare.

Prepare your hearts for Death's cold hand! prepare
Your souls for flight, your bodies for the earth!
Prepare your arms for glorious victory!
Prepare your eyes to meet a holy God!
        Prepare, prepare.

Whose fatal scroll is that? Methinks 'tis mine!
Why sinks my heart, why faultereth my tongue?
Had I three lives, I'd die in such a cause,
And rise, with ghosts, over the well-fought field.
        Prepare, prepare.

The arrows of Almighty God are drawn!
Angels of Death stand in the low'ring heavens!
Thousands of souls must seek the realms of light,
And walk together on the clouds of heaven!
        Prepare, prepare.

Soldiers, prepare! Our cause is Heaven's cause;
Soldiers, prepare! Be worthy of our cause:
Prepare to meet our fathers in the sky:
Prepare, O troops, that are to fall today!
        Prepare, prepare.

Alfred shall smile, and make his harp rejoice;
The Norman William, and the learned Clerk,
And Lion-Heart, and black-brow'd Edward, with
His loyal queen shall rise, and welcome us!
                Prepare, prepare.

SONG 1ST BY A SHEPHERD

Welcome stranger to this place,
Where joy doth sit on every bough,
Paleness flies from every face,
We reap not, what we do not sow.

Innocence doth like a Rose,
Bloom on every Maiden's cheek;
Honor twines around her brows,
The jewel Health adorns her neck.

SONG 3D BY AN OLD SHEPHERD

When silver snow decks Sylvio's clothes
And jewel hangs at shepherd's nose,
We can abide life's pelting storm
That makes our limbs quake, if our hearts be warm.

Whilst Virtue is our walking staff,
And Truth a lantern to our path;
We can abide life's pelting storm
That makes our limbs quake, if our hearts be warm.

Blow boisterous Wind, stern Winter frown,
Innocence is a Winter's gown;
So clad, we'll abide life's pelting storm
That makes our limbs quake, if our hearts be warm.

Songs of
Innocence

INTRODUCTION

Piping down the valleys wild
Piping songs of pleasant glee
On a cloud I saw a child,
And he laughing said to me.

Pipe a song about a Lamb;
So I piped with merry cheer,
Piper pipe that song again—
So I piped, he wept to hear.

Drop thy pipe thy happy pipe
Sing thy songs of happy cheer,
So I sung the same again
While he wept with joy to hear.

Piper sit thee down and write
In a book that all may read—
So he vanish'd from my sight.
And I pluck'd a hollow reed.

And I made a rural pen,
And I stain'd the water clear,
And I wrote my happy songs
Every child may joy to hear.

THE SHEPHERD

How sweet is the Shepherd's sweet lot,
From the morn to the evening he strays:
He shall follow his sheep all the day
And his tongue shall be filled with praise.

For he hears the lambs innocent call,
And he hears the ewes tender reply,
He is watchful while they are in peace,
For they know when their Shepherd is nigh.

THE ECHOING GREEN

The Sun does arise,
And make happy the skies.
The merry bells ring
To welcome the Spring.
The skylark and thrush,
The birds of the bush,
Sing louder around,
To the bells cheerful sound.
While our sports shall be seen
On the Echoing Green.

Old John with white hair
Does laugh away care,
Sitting under the oak,
Among the old folk,
They laugh at our play,
And soon they all say.
Such such were the joys.
When we all girls & boys,
In our youth-time were seen,
On the Echoing Green.

Till the little ones weary
No more can be merry;
The sun does descend,
And our sports have an end.
Round the laps of their mothers,
Many sisters and brothers,
Like birds in their nest,
Are ready for rest;
And sport no more seen,
On the darkening Green.

THE LAMB

Little Lamb who made thee
Dost thou know who made thee
Gave thee life & bid thee feed
By the stream & o'er the mead;
Gave thee clothing of delight,
Softest clothing wooly bright;
Gave thee such a tender voice,
Making all the vales rejoice!
Little Lamb who made thee
Dost thou know who made thee
Little Lamb I'll tell thee,
Little Lamb I'll tell thee!
He is called by thy name,
For he calls himself a Lamb:
He is meek & he is mild,
He became a little child:
I a child & thou a lamb,
We are called by his name.
Little Lamb God bless thee.
Little Lamb God bless thee.

THE LITTLE BLACK BOY

My mother bore me in the southern wild,
And I am black, but O! my soul is white;
White as an angel is the English child:
But I am black as if bereav'd of light.

My mother taught me underneath a tree
And sitting down before the heat of day,
She took me on her lap and kissed me,
And pointing to the east began to say.

Look on the rising sun: there God does live
And gives his light, and gives his heat away.
And flowers and trees and beasts and men receive
Comfort in morning, joy in the noonday.

And we are put on earth a little space,
That we may learn to bear the beams of love,
And these black bodies and this sunburnt face
Is but a cloud, and like a shady grove.

For when our souls have learn'd the heat to bear
The cloud will vanish, we shall hear his voice,
Saying: come out from the grove my love & care,
And round my golden tent like lambs rejoice.

Thus did my mother say and kissed me,
And thus I say to little English boy.
When I from black and he from white cloud free,
And round the tent of God like lambs we joy:

I'll shade him from the heat till he can bear,
To lean in joy upon our father's knee.
And then I'll stand and stroke his silver hair,
And be like him and he will then love me.

THE BLOSSOM

Merry Merry Sparrow
Under leaves so green
A happy Blossom
Sees you swift as arrow
Seek your cradle narrow
Near my Bosom.

Pretty Pretty Robin
Under leaves so green
A happy Blossom
Hears you sobbing sobbing
Pretty Pretty Robin
Near my Bosom.

THE CHIMNEY SWEEPER

When my mother died I was very young,
And my father sold me while yet my tongue,
Could scarcely cry weep weep weep weep.
So your chimneys I sweep & in soot I sleep.

There's little Tom Dacre, who cried when his head
That curl'd like a lamb's back, was shav'd, so I said:
Hush Tom never mind it, for when your head's bare,
You know that the soot cannot spoil your white hair.

And so he was quiet, & that very night,
As Tom was a-sleeping he had such a sight,
That thousands of sweepers Dick, Joe, Ned & Jack
Were all of them lock'd up in coffins of black.

And by came an Angel who had a bright key,
And he open'd the coffins & set them all free.
Then down a green plain leaping laughing they run
And wash in a river and shine in the Sun.

Then naked & white, all their bags left behind,
They rise upon clouds, and sport in the wind.
And the Angel told Tom if he'd be a good boy,
He'd have God for his father & never want joy.

And so Tom awoke and we rose in the dark
And got with our bags & our brushes to work.
Tho' the morning was cold, Tom was happy & warm,
So if all do their duty, they need not fear harm.

THE LITTLE BOY LOST

Father, father, where are you going
O do not walk so fast.
Speak father, speak to your little boy
Or else I shall be lost.

The night was dark, no father was there
The child was wet with dew.
The mire was deep, & the child did weep
And away the vapor flew.

THE LITTLE BOY FOUND

The little boy lost in the lonely fen,
Led by the wand'ring light,
Began to cry, but God ever nigh,
Appeared like his father in white.

He kissed the child & by the hand led
And to his mother brought,
Who in sorrow pale, thro' the lonely dale
Her little boy weeping sought.

LAUGHING SONG

When the green woods laugh, with the voice of joy
And the dimpling stream runs laughing by,
When the air does laugh with our merry wit,
And the green hill laughs with the noise of it.

When the meadows laugh with lively green
And the grasshopper laughs in the merry scene,
When Mary and Susan and Emily,
With their sweet round mouths sing Ha, Ha, He.

When the painted birds laugh in the shade
Where our table with cherries and nuts is spread,
Come live & be merry and join with me,
To sing the sweet chorus of Ha, Ha, He.

A CRADLE SONG

Sweet dreams form a shade,
O'er my lovely infant's head.
Sweet dreams of pleasant streams,
By happy silent moony beams.

Sweet sleep with soft down,
Weave thy brows an infant crown.
Sweet sleep Angel mild,
Hover o'er my happy child.

Sweet smiles in the night,
Hover over my delight.
Sweet smiles, Mother's smiles
All the livelong night beguiles.

Sweet moans, dovelike sighs,
Chase not slumber from thy eyes.
Sweet moans, sweeter smiles,
All the dovelike moans beguiles.

Sleep sleep happy child.
All creation slept and smil'd.
Sleep sleep, happy sleep,
While o'er thee thy mother weep.

Sweet babe in thy face,
Holy image I can trace.
Sweet babe once like thee,
Thy maker lay and wept for me

Wept for me, for thee, for all,
When he was an infant small.

Thou his image ever see,
Heavenly face that smiles on thee.

Smiles on thee, on me, on all,
Who became an infant small,
Infant smiles are his own smiles.
Heaven & earth to peace beguiles.

THE DIVINE IMAGE

To Mercy Pity Peace and Love,
All pray in their distress:
And to these virtues of delight
Return their thankfulness.

For Mercy Pity Peace and Love,
Is God our father dear:
And Mercy Pity Peace and Love,
Is Man, his child and care.

For Mercy has a human heart
Pity, a human face:
And Love, the human form divine,
And Peace, the human dress.

Then every man of every clime,
That prays in his distress,
Prays to the human form divine
Love Mercy Pity Peace.

And all must love the human form,
In heathen, Turk or Jew.
Where Mercy, Love & Pity dwell,
There God is dwelling too.

HOLY THURSDAY

'Twas on a Holy Thursday their innocent faces clean,
The children walking two & two in red & blue & green;
Gray-headed beadles walked before with wands as white as
    snow,
Till into the high dome of Paul's they like Thames' waters
    flow.

O what a multitude they seem'd, these flowers of London
    town
Seated in companies they sit with radiance all their own.
The hum of multitudes was there but multitudes of lambs,
Thousands of little boys & girls raising their innocent
    hands.

Now like a mighty wind they raise to heaven the voice of
    song
Or like harmonious thunderings the seats of heaven among.
Beneath them sit the aged men, wise guardians of the poor.
Then cherish pity, lest you drive an angel from your door.

NIGHT

The sun descending in the west.
The evening star does shine.
The birds are silent in their nest,
And I must seek for mine,
The moon like a flower,
In heaven's high bower;
With silent delight,
Sits and smiles on the night.

Farewell green fields and happy groves,
Where flocks have took delight;
Where lambs have nibbled, silent moves
The feet of angels bright;
Unseen they pour blessing,
And joy without ceasing,
On each bud and blossom,
And each sleeping bosom.

They look in every thoughtless nest,
Where birds are covered warm;
They visit caves of every beast,
To keep them all from harm;
If they see any weeping,
That should have been sleeping
They pour sleep on their head
And sit down by their bed.

When wolves and tygers howl for prey
They pitying stand and weep;
Seeking to drive their thirst away,
And keep them from the sheep.

But if they rush dreadful;
The angels most heedful,
Receive each mild spirit,
New worlds to inherit.

And there the lion's ruddy eyes,
Shall flow with tears of gold:
And pitying the tender cries,
And walking round the fold:
Saying: wrath by his meekness
And by his health, sickness,
Is driven away,
From our immortal day.

And now beside thee bleating lamb,
I can lie down and sleep;
Or think on him who bore thy name,
Graze after thee and weep.
For wash'd in life's river,
My bright mane forever,
Shall shine like the gold,
As I guard o'er the fold.

SPRING

Sound the Flute!
Now it's mute.
Birds delight
Day and Night.
Nightingale
In the dale
Lark in Sky
Merrily
Merrily Merrily to welcome in the Year.

Little Boy
Full of joy.
Little Girl
Sweet and small,
Cock does crow
So do you.
Merry voice
Infant noise
Merrily Merrily to welcome in the Year.

Little Lamb
Here I am,
Come and lick
My white neck.
Let me pull
Your soft Wool.
Let me kiss
Your soft face.
Merrily Merrily we welcome in the Year.

NURSE'S SONG

When the voices of children are heard on the green
And laughing is heard on the hill,
My heart is at rest within my breast
And everything else is still.

Then come home my children, the sun is gone down
And the dews of night arise;
Come come leave off play, and let us away
Till the morning appears in the skies.

No no let us play, for it is yet day
And we cannot go to sleep;
Besides in the sky, the little birds fly
And the hills are all covered with sheep.

Well well go & play till the light fades away
And then go home to bed.
The little ones leaped & shouted & laugh'd
And all the hills echoed.

INFANT JOY

"I have no name
I am but two days old."
What shall I call thee?
"I happy am
Joy is my name."
Sweet joy befall thee!

Pretty joy!
Sweet joy but two days old,
Sweet joy I call thee;
Thou dost smile.
I sing the while
Sweet joy befall thee.

A DREAM

Once a dream did weave a shade,
O'er my Angel-guarded bed,
That an Emmet lost it's way
Where on grass methought I lay.

Troubled, 'wilder'd and folorn
Dark, benighted, travel-worn,
Over many a tangled spray
All heartbroke I heard her say.

O my children! do they cry
Do they hear their father sigh?
Now they look abroad to see,
Now return and weep for me.

Pitying I dropp'd a tear:
But I saw a glowworm near,
Who replied: What wailing wight
Calls the watchman of the night?

I am set to light the ground,
While the beetle goes his round:
Follow now the beetle's hum,
Little wanderer hie thee home.

ON ANOTHER'S SORROW

Can I see another's woe,
And not be in sorrow too.
Can I see another's grief,
And not seek for kind relief.

Can I see a falling tear,
And not feel my sorrow's share,
Can a father see his child,
Weep, nor be with sorrow fill'd.

Can a mother sit and hear,
An infant groan an infant fear—
No no never can it be.
Never never can it be.

And can he who smiles on all
Hear the wren with sorrows small,
Hear the small bird's grief & care
Hear the woes that infants bear—

And not sit beside the nest
Pouring pity in their breast,
And not sit the cradle near
Weeping tear on infant's tear.

And not sit both night & day,
Wiping all our tears away.
O! no never can it be.
Never never can it be.

He doth give his joy to all.
He becomes an infant small.
He becomes a man of woe
He doth feel the sorrow too.

Think not, thou canst sigh a sigh,
And thy maker is not by.
Think not, thou canst weep a tear,
And thy maker is not near.

O! he gives to us his joy,
That our grief he may destroy
Till our grief is fled & gone
He doth sit by us and moan

Songs of
Experience

INTRODUCTION

Hear the voice of the Bard!
Who Present, Past, & Future sees
Whose ears have heard,
The Holy Word,
That walk'd among the ancient trees.

Calling the lapsed Soul
And weeping in the evening dew:
That might control,
The starry pole;
And fallen fallen light renew!

O Earth O Earth return!
Arise from out the dewy grass;
Night is worn,
And the morn
Rises from the slumberous mass.

Turn away no more:
Why wilt thou turn away
The starry floor
The wat'ry shore
Is giv'n thee till the break of day.

EARTH'S ANSWER

Earth rais'd up her head,
From the darkness dread & drear.
Her light fled:
Stony dread!
And her locks cover'd with gray despair.

Prison'd on wat'ry shore
Starry Jealousy does keep my den
Cold and hoar
Weeping o'er
I hear the Father of the ancient men.

Selfish father of men
Cruel jealous selfish fear
Can delight
Chain'd in night
The virgins of youth and morning bear.

Does spring hide its joy
When buds and blossoms grow?
Does the sower
Sow by night?
Or the plowman in darkness plow?

Break this heavy chain,
That does freeze my bones around
Selfish! vain!
Eternal bane!
That free Love with bondage bound.

THE CLOD & THE PEBBLE

Love seeketh not Itself to please,
Nor for itself hath any care;
But for another gives its ease,
And builds a Heaven in Hell's despair.

So sang a little Clod of Clay,
Trodden with the cattle's feet:
But a Pebble of the brook,
Warbled out these meters meet.

Love seeketh only Self to please,
To bind another to Its delight:
Joys in another's loss of ease,
And builds a Hell in Heaven's despite.

HOLY THURSDAY

Is this a holy thing to see,
In a rich and fruitful land,
Babes reduced to misery,
Fed with cold and usurous hand?

Is that trembling cry a song?
Can it be a song of joy?
And so many children poor?
It is a land of poverty!

And their sun does never shine.
And their fields are bleak & bare.
And their ways are fill'd with thorns.
It is eternal winter there.

For where-e'er the sun does shine,
And where-e'er the rain does fall:
Babe can never hunger there,
Nor poverty the mind appall.

THE LITTLE GIRL LOST

In futurity
I prophetic see,
That the earth from sleep,
(Grave the sentence deep)

Shall arise and seek
For her maker meek:
And the desert wild
Become a garden mild.

———————

In the southern clime,
Where the summer's prime,
Never fades away;
Lovely Lyca lay.

Seven summers old
Lovely Lyca told,
She had wandered long,
Hearing wild birds' song.

Sweet sleep come to me
Underneath this tree;
Do father, mother weep—
Where can Lyca sleep.

Lost in desert wild
Is your little child.
How can Lyca sleep,
If her mother weep.

If her heart does ache,
Then let Lyca wake;
If my mother sleep,
Lyca shall not weep.

Frowning frowning night,
O'er this desert bright,
Let thy moon arise,
While I close my eyes.

Sleeping Lyca lay;
While the beasts of prey,
Come from caverns deep,
View'd the maid asleep

The kingly lion stood
And the virgin view'd,
Then he gamboled round
O'er the hallowed ground;

Leopards, tygers play,
Round her as she lay;
While the lion old,
Bow'd his mane of gold.

And her bosom lick,
And upon her neck,
From his eyes of flame,
Ruby tears there came;

While the lioness,
Loos'd her slender dress,
And naked they convey'd
To caves the sleeping maid.

THE LITTLE GIRL FOUND

All the night in woe,
Lyca's parents go:
Over valleys deep,
While the deserts weep.

Tired and woebegone,
Hoarse with making moan:
Arm in arm seven days,
They trac'd the desert ways.

Seven nights they sleep,
Among shadows deep:
And dream they see their child
Starv'd in desert wild.

Pale thro' pathless ways
The fancied image strays,
Famish'd, weeping, weak
With hollow piteous shriek

Rising from unrest,
The trembling woman pressed,
With feet of weary woe;
She could no further go.

In his arms he bore,
Her arm'd with sorrow sore;
Till before their way,
A couching lion lay.

Turning back was vain,
Soon his heavy mane,

Bore them to the ground;
Then he stalk'd around,

Smelling to his prey.
But their fears allay,
When he licks their hands;
And silent by them stands.

They look upon his eyes
Fill'd with deep surprise:
And wondering behold,
A spirit arm'd in gold.

On his head a crown
On his shoulders down
Flow'd his golden hair.
Gone was all their care.

Follow me he said,
Weep not for the maid;
In my palace deep,
Lyca lies asleep.

Then they followed,
Where the vision led:
And saw their sleeping child,
Among tygers wild.

To this day they dwell
In a lonely dell
Nor fear the wolvish howl,
Nor the lions' growl.

THE CHIMNEY SWEEPER

A little black thing among the snow:
Crying weep, weep, in notes of woe!
Where are thy father & mother? say?
They are both gone up to the church to pray.

Because I was happy upon the heath,
And smil'd among the winter's snow:
They clothed me in the clothes of death,
And taught me to sing the notes of woe.

And because I am happy, & dance & sing,
They think they have done me no injury:
And are gone to praise God & his Priest & King
Who make up a heaven of our misery.

NURSE'S SONG

When the voices of children are heard on the green
And whisperings are in the dale:
The days of my youth rise fresh in my mind,
My face turns green and pale.

Then come home my children, the sun is gone down
And the dews of night arise
Your spring & your day, are wasted in play
And your winter and night in disguise.

THE SICK ROSE

O Rose thou art sick.
The invisible worm,
That flies in the night
In the howling storm:

Has found out thy bed
Of crimson joy:
And his dark secret love
Does thy life destroy.

THE FLY

Little Fly
Thy summer's play,
My thoughtless hand
Has brush'd away.

Am not I
A fly like thee?
Or art not thou
A man like me?

For I dance
And drink & sing:
Till some blind hand
Shall brush my wing.

If thought is life
And strength & breath:
And the want
Of thought is death;

Then am I
A happy fly,
If I live,
Or if I die.

THE ANGEL

I Dreamt a Dream! what can it mean?
And that I was a maiden Queen:
Guarded by an Angel mild:
Witless woe, was ne'er beguil'd!

And I wept both night and day
And he wip'd my tears away
And I wept both day and night
And hid from him my heart's delight.

So he took his wings and fled:
Then the morn blush'd rosy red:
I dried my tears & armed my fears,
With ten thousand shields and spears.

Soon my Angel came again;
I was arm'd, he came in vain:
For the time of youth was fled
And gray hairs were on my head.

THE TYGER

Tyger Tyger, burning bright,
In the forests of the night;
What immortal hand or eye,
Could frame thy fearful symmetry?

In what distant deeps or skies
Burnt the fire of thine eyes?
On what wings dare he aspire?
What the hand dare seize the fire?

And what shoulder, & what art,
Could twist the sinews of thy heart?
And when thy heart began to beat,
What dread hand? & what dread feet?

What the hammer? what the chain,
In what furnace was thy brain?
What the anvil? what dread grasp
Dare its deadly terrors clasp!

When the stars threw down their spears
And water'd heaven with their tears:
Did he smile his work to see?
Did he who made the Lamb make thee?

Tyger Tyger burning bright,
In the forests of the night:
What immortal hand or eye,
Dare frame thy fearful symmetry?

MY PRETTY ROSE TREE

A flower was offered to me;
Such a flower as May never bore.
But I said I've a Pretty Rose Tree:
And I passed the sweet flower o'er.

Then I went to my Pretty Rose Tree;
To tend her by day and by night.
But my Rose turned away with jealousy:
And her thorns were my only delight.

AH! SUNFLOWER

Ah Sunflower! weary of time,
Who countest the steps of the Sun:
Seeking after that sweet golden clime
Where the traveler's journey is done.

Where the Youth pined away with desire,
And the pale Virgin shrouded in snow:
Arise from their graves and aspire,
Where my Sunflower wishes to go.

THE LILY

The modest Rose puts forth a thorn:
The humble Sheep, a threatening horn:
While the Lily white, shall in Love delight,
Nor a thorn nor a threat stain her beauty bright.

THE GARDEN OF LOVE

I went to the Garden of Love,
And saw what I never had seen:
A Chapel was built in the midst,
Where I used to play on the green.

And the gates of this Chapel were shut,
And "Thou shalt not" writ over the door;
So I turn'd to the Garden of Love,
That so many sweet flowers bore.

And I saw it was filled with graves,
And tombstones where flowers should be:
And Priests in black gowns, were walking their rounds,
And binding with briars, my joys & desires.

THE LITTLE VAGABOND

Dear Mother, dear Mother, the Church is cold,
But the Alehouse is healthy & pleasant & warm;
Besides I can tell where I am used well,
Such usage in heaven will never do well.

But if at the Church they would give us some Ale.
And a pleasant fire, our souls to regale;
We'd sing and we'd pray, all the livelong day;
Nor ever once wish from the Church to stray.

Then the Parson might preach & drink & sing.
And we'd be as happy as birds in the spring:
And modest dame Lurch, who is always at Church,
Would not have bandy children nor fasting nor birch.

And God like a father rejoicing to see,
His children as pleasant and happy as he:
Would have no more quarrel with the Devil or the
        Barrel
But kiss him & give him both drink and apparel.

LONDON

I wander thro' each charter'd street,
Near where the charter'd Thames does flow.
And mark in every face I meet
Marks of weakness, marks of woe.

In every cry of every Man,
In every Infant's cry of fear,
In every voice: in every ban,
The mind-forg'd manacles I hear

How the Chimney-sweepers cry
Every black'ning Church appalls,
And the hapless Soldier's sigh
Runs in blood down Palace walls

But most thro' midnight streets I hear
How the youthful Harlot's curse
Blasts the newborn Infant's tear
And blights with plagues the Marriage hearse.

THE HUMAN ABSTRACT

Pity would be no more,
If we did not make somebody Poor:
And Mercy no more could be,
If all were as happy as we;

And mutual fear brings peace;
Till the selfish loves increase.
Then Cruelty knits a snare,
And spreads his baits with care.

He sits down with holy fears,
And waters the ground with tears:
Then Humility takes its root
Underneath his foot.

Soon spreads the dismal shade
Of Mystery over his head;
And the Caterpillar and Fly,
Feed on the Mystery.

And it bears the fruit of Deceit,
Ruddy and sweet to eat;
And the Raven his nest has made
In its thickest shade.

The Gods of the earth and sea,
Sought thro' Nature to find this Tree
But their search was all in vain:
There grows one in the Human Brain.

INFANT SORROW

My mother groaned! my father wept.
Into the dangerous world I leapt:
Helpless, naked, piping loud;
Like a fiend hid in a cloud.

Struggling in my father's hands:
Striving against my swaddling bands:
Bound and weary I thought best
To sulk upon my mother's breast.

A POISON TREE

I was angry with my friend;
I told my wrath, my wrath did end.
I was angry with my foe:
I told it not, my wrath did grow.

And I watered it in fears,
Night & morning with my tears:
And I sunned it with smiles,
And with soft deceitful wiles.

And it grew both day and night.
Till it bore an apple bright.
And my foe beheld it shine,
And he knew that it was mine.

And into my garden stole,
When the night had veiled the pole;
In the morning glad I see;
My foe outstretched beneath the tree.

A LITTLE BOY LOST

Naught loves another as itself
Nor venerates another so.
Nor is it possible to Thought
A greater than itself to know:

And Father, how can I love you,
Or any of my brothers more?
I love you like the little bird
That picks up crumbs around the door.

The Priest sat by and heard the child.
In trembling zeal he seiz'd his hair:
He led him by his little coat:
And all admir'd the Priestly care.

And standing on the altar high,
Lo what a fiend is here! said he:
One who sets reason up for judge
Of our most holy Mystery.

The weeping child could not be heard.
The weeping parents wept in vain:
They stripp'd him to his little shirt.
And bound him in an iron chain.

And burn'd him in a holy place,
Where many had been burn'd before:
The weeping parents wept in vain.
Are such things done on Albion's shore.

A LITTLE GIRL LOST

Children of the future Age,
Reading this indignant page;
Know that in a former time.
Love! sweet Love! was thought a crime.

In the Age of Gold,
Free from winter's cold:
Youth and maiden bright,
To the holy light,
Naked in the sunny beams delight.

Once a youthful pair
Fill'd with softest care:
Met in garden bright,
Where the holy light,
Had just removed the curtains of the night.

There in rising day,
On the grass they play:
Parents were afar:
Strangers came not near:
And the maiden soon forgot her fear.

Tired with kisses sweet
They agree to meet,
When the silent sleep
Waves o'er heavens deep;
And the weary tired wanderers weep.

To her father white
Came the maiden bright:

But his loving look,
Like the holy book,
All her tender limbs with terror shook.

Ona! pale and weak!
To thy father speak:
O the trembling fear!
O the dismal care!
That shakes the blossoms of my hoary hair.

TO TIRZAH

Whate'er is Born of Mortal Birth,
Must be consumed with the Earth
To rise from Generation free;
Then what have I to do with thee?

The Sexes sprung from Shame & Pride
Blow'd in the morn: in evening died
But Mercy changed Death into Sleep;
The Sexes rose to work & weep.

Thou Mother of my Mortal part.
With cruelty didst mold my Heart.
And with false self-deceiving tears,
Didst bind my Nostrils Eyes & Ears.

Didst close my Tongue in senseless clay
And me to Mortal Life betray:
The Death of Jesus set me free,
Then what have I to do with thee?

THE SCHOOL BOY

I love to rise in a summer morn,
When the birds sing on every tree;
The distant huntsman winds his horn,
And the skylark sings with me.
O! what sweet company.

But to go to school in a summer morn,
O! it drives all joy away;
Under a cruel eye outworn,
The little ones spend the day,
In sighing and dismay.

Ah! then at times I drooping sit,
And spend many an anxious hour.
Nor in my book can I take delight,
Nor sit in learning's bower,
Worn thro' with the dreary shower.

How can the bird that is born for joy,
Sit in a cage and sing.
How can a child when fears annoy,
But droop his tender wing,
And forget his youthful spring.

O! father & mother, if buds are nipp'd,
And blossoms blown away,
And if the tender plants are stripp'd
Of their joy in the springing day,
By sorrow and cares dismay,

How shall the summer arise in joy.
Or the summer fruits appear,
Or how shall we gather what griefs destroy
Or bless the mellowing year,
When the blasts of winter appear.

THE VOICE OF THE ANCIENT BARD

Youth of delight come hither:
And see the opening morn,
Image of truth newborn.
Doubt is fled & clouds of reason.
Dark disputes & artful teasing.
Folly is an endless maze,
Tangled roots perplex her ways,
How many have fallen there!
They stumble all night over bones of the dead;
And feel they know not what but care;
And wish to lead others when they should be led.

A DIVINE IMAGE

[AN EARLY SONG OF EXPERIENCE INCLUDED
IN ONE LATE COPY]

Cruelty has a Human Heart
And Jealousy a Human Face
Terror, the Human Form Divine
And Secrecy, the Human Dress.

The Human Dress, is forged Iron
The Human Form, a fiery Forge.
The Human Face, a Furnace seal'd
The Human Heart, its hungry Gorge.

From the
Rossetti
Manuscript

Never seek to tell thy love
Love that never told can be;
For the gentle wind does move
Silently, invisibly.

I told my love, I told my love,
I told her all my heart,
Trembling, cold, in ghastly fears—
Ah, she doth depart.

Soon as she was gone from me
A traveler came by
Silently, invisibly—
O, was no deny.

I laid me down upon a bank
Where love lay sleeping.
I heard among the rushes dank
Weeping, Weeping.

Then I went to the heath & the wild
To the thistles & thorns of the waste
And they told me how they were beguil'd,
Driven out, & compell'd to be chaste.

I saw a chapel all of gold
That none did dare to enter in,
And many weeping stood without,
Weeping, mourning, worshipping.

I saw a serpent rise between
The white pillars of the door,
And he forc'd & forc'd & forc'd,
Down the golden hinges tore.

And along the pavement sweet,
Set with pearls & rubies bright,
All his slimy length he drew,
Till upon the altar white

Vomiting his poison out
On the bread & on the wine.
So I turn'd into a sty
And laid me down among the swine.

I asked a thief to steal me a peach:
He turned up his eyes.
I ask'd a lithe lady to lie her down:
Holy & meek she cries.

As soon as I went an angel came:
He wink'd at the thief
And smil'd at the dame,
And without one word spoke
Had a peach from the tree,
And 'twixt earnest & joke
Enjoy'd the Lady.

I heard an Angel singing
When the day was springing,
"Mercy, Pity, Peace
Is the world's release."

Thus he sung all day
Over the new mown hay,
Till the sun went down
And haycocks looked brown.

I heard a Devil curse
Over the heath & the furze,
"Mercy could be no more,
If there was nobody poor,

"And pity no more could be,
If all were as happy as we."
At his curse the sun went down,
And the heavens gave a frown.

Down pour'd the heavy rain
Over the new reap'd grain,
And Miseries' increase
Is Mercy, Pity, Peace.

A CRADLE SONG

Sleep, Sleep, beauty bright
Dreaming o'er the joys of night.
Sleep, Sleep: in thy sleep
Little sorrows sit & weep.

Sweet Babe, in thy face
Soft desires I can trace
Secret joys & secret smiles
Little pretty infant wiles.

As thy softest limbs I feel
Smiles as of the morning steal
O'er thy cheek & o'er thy breast
Where thy little heart does rest.

O, the cunning wiles that creep
In thy little heart asleep.
When thy little heart does wake,
Then the dreadful lightnings break.

From thy cheek & from thy eye
O'er the youthful harvests nigh
Infant wiles & infant smiles
Heaven & Earth of peace beguiles.

INFANT SORROW

My mother groan'd, my father wept;
Into the dangerous world I leapt,
Helpless, naked, piping loud,
Like a fiend hid in a cloud.

Struggling in my father's hands
Striving against my swaddling bands,
Bound & weary, I thought best
To sulk upon my mother's breast.

When I saw that rage was vain,
And to sulk would nothing gain,
Turning many a trick & wile,
I began to soothe & smile.

And I sooth'd day after day
Till upon the ground I stray;
And I smil'd night after night,
Seeking only for delight.

And I saw before me shine
Clusters of the wand'ring vine,
And many a lovely flower & tree
Stretch'd their blossoms out to me.

My father then with holy look,
In his hands a holy book,
Pronounc'd curses on my head
And bound me in a myrtle shade.

IN A MYRTLE SHADE

Why should I be bound to thee,
O my lovely myrtle tree?
Love, free love, cannot be bound
To any tree that grows on ground.

O, how sick & weary I
Underneath my myrtle lie,
Like to dung upon the ground
Underneath my myrtle bound.

Oft my myrtle sigh'd in vain
To behold my heavy chain;
Oft my father saw us sigh,
And laugh'd at our simplicity.

So I smote him & his gore
Stain'd the roots my myrtle bore.
But the time of youth is fled,
And gray hairs are on my head.

Silent, Silent Night
Quench the holy light
Of thy torches bright.

For possess'd of Day
Thousand spirits stray
That sweet joys betray

Why should joys be sweet
Used with deceit
Nor with sorrows meet?

But an honest joy
Does itself destroy
For a harlot coy.

O lapwing, thou fliest around the heath,
Nor seest the net that is spread beneath.
Why dost thou not fly among the corn fields?
They cannot spread nets where a harvest yields.

Thou hast a lap full of seed,
And this is a fine country.
Why dost thou not cast thy seed
And live in it merrily?

Shall I cast it on the sand
And turn it into fruitful land?

For on no other ground
Can I sow my seed
Without tearing up
Some stinking weed.

TO NOBODADDY

Why art thou silent & invisible,
Father of Jealousy?
Why dost thou hide thy self in clouds
From every searching Eye?

Why darkness & obscurity
In all thy words & laws,
That none dare eat the fruit but from
The wily serpent's jaws?
Or is it because Secrecy gains females' loud applause?

Are not the joys of morning sweeter
Than the joys of night?
And are the vig'rous joys of youth
Ashamed of the light?

Let age & sickness silent rob
The vineyards in the night;
But those who burn with vig'rous youth
Pluck fruits before the light.

Love to faults is always blind,
Always is to joy inclin'd,
Lawless, wing'd, & unconfin'd,
And breaks all chains from every mind.

Deceit to secrecy confin'd,
Lawful, cautious, & refin'd;
To everything but interest blind,
And forges fetters for the mind.

THE WILDFLOWER'S SONG

As I wander'd the forest,
The green leaves among,
I heard a wildflower
Singing a song:

"I slept in the dark
In the silent night,
I murmur'd my fears
And I felt delight.

"In the morning I went
As rosy as morn
To seek for new Joy,
But I met with scorn."

SOFT SNOW

I walked abroad in a snowy day:
I ask'd the soft snow with me to play:
She play'd & she melted in all her prime,
And the winter call'd it a dreadful crime.

AN ANCIENT PROVERB

Remove away that black'ning church:
Remove away that marriage hearse:
Remove away that place of blood:
You'll quite remove the ancient curse.

TO MY MYRTLE

To a lovely myrtle bound,
Blossoms show'ring all around,
Oh, how sick & weary I
Underneath my myrtle lie.
Why should I be bound to thee,
O, my lovely myrtle tree?

MERLIN'S PROPHECY

The harvest shall flourish in wintry weather
When two virginities meet together:

The King & the Priest must be tied in a tether
Before two virgins can meet together.

DAY

The Sun arises in the East,
Cloth'd in robes of blood & gold;
Swords & spears & wrath increased
All around his bosom roll'd,
Crown'd with warlike fires & raging desires.

THE MARRIAGE RING

"Come hither my sparrows,
My little arrows.
If a tear or a smile
Will a man beguile,
If an amorous delay
Clouds a sunshiny day,
If the step of a foot
Smites the heart to its root,
'Tis the marriage ring
Makes each fairy a king."

So a fairy sung.
From the leaves I sprung.
He leap'd from the spray
To flee away.
But in my hat caught
He soon shall be taught.
Let him laugh, let him cry,
He's my butterfly;
For I've pull'd out the sting
Of the marriage ring.

The sword sung on the barren heath,
The sickle in the fruitful field:
The sword he sung a song of death,
But could not make the sickle yield.

Abstinence sows sand all over
The ruddy limbs & flaming hair,
But Desire Gratified
Plants fruits of life & beauty there.

In a wife I would desire
What in whores is always found—
The lineaments of Gratified desire.

If you trap the moment before it's ripe,
The tears of repentance you'll certainly wipe;
But if once you let the ripe moment go
You can never wipe off the tears of woe.

ETERNITY

He who binds to himself a joy
Does the winged life destroy;
But he who kisses the joy as it flies
Lives in eternity's sunrise.

THE QUESTION ANSWER'D

What is it men in women do require?
The lineaments of Gratified Desire.
What is it women do in men require?
The lineaments of Gratified Desire.

LACEDEMONIAN INSTRUCTION

"Come hither, my boy, tell me what thou seest there."
"A fool tangled in a religious snare."

RICHES

The countless gold of a merry heart,
The rubies & pearls of a loving eye,
The indolent never can bring to the mart,
Nor the secret hoard up in his treasury.

AN ANSWER TO THE PARSON

"Why of the sheep do you not learn peace?"
"Because I don't want you to shear my fleece."

The look of love alarms
Because 'tis fill'd with fire;
But the look of soft deceit
Shall win the lover's hire.

Which are beauties sweetest dress?
Soft deceit & idleness,
These are beauties sweetest dress.

MOTTO TO THE SONGS OF INNOCENCE & OF EXPERIENCE

The Good are attracted by Men's perceptions,
And think not for themselves;
Till Experience teaches them to catch
And to cage the Fairies & Elves.

And then the Knave begins to snarl
And the Hypocrite to howl;
And all his good Friends show their private ends,
And the Eagle is known from the Owl.

"Let the Brothels of Paris be opened
With many an alluring dance
To awake the Pestilence thro' the city,"
Said the beautiful Queen of France.

The King awoke on his couch of gold,
As soon as he heard these tidings told:
"Arise & come, both fife & drum,
And the Famine shall eat both crust & crumb."

Then he swore a great & solemn Oath:
"To kill the people I am loth,
But if they rebel, they must go to hell:
They shall have a Priest & a passing bell."

Then old Nobodaddy aloft
Farted & belch'd & cough'd,
And said, "I love hanging & drawing & quartering
Every bit as well as war & slaughtering.
Damn praying & singing,
Unless they will bring in
The blood of ten thousand by fighting or swinging."

The Queen of France just touched this Globe,
And the Pestilence darted from her robe;
But our good Queen quite grows to the ground,
And a great many suckers grow all around.

Fayette beside King Lewis stood;
He saw him sign his hand;
And soon he saw the famine rage
About the fruitful land.

Fayette beheld the Queen to smile
And wink her lovely eye;
And soon he saw the pestilence
From street to street to fly.

Fayette beheld the King & Queen
In tears & iron bound;
But mute Fayette wept tear for tear,
And guarded them around.

Fayette, Fayette, thou'rt bought & sold,
And sold is thy happy morrow;
Thou gavest the tears of Pity away
In exchange for the tears of sorrow.

Who will exchange his own fireside
For the steps of another's door?
Who will exchange his wheaten loaf
For the links of a dungeon floor?

O, who would smile on the wintry seas,
& Pity the stormy roar?
Or who will exchange his newborn child
For the dog at the wintry door?

When Klopstock England defied,
Uprose William Blake in his pride;
For old Nobodaddy aloft
Farted & Belch'd & cough'd;
Then swore a great oath that made heaven quake,
And call'd aloud to English Blake.
Blake was giving his body ease
At Lambeth beneath the poplar trees.
From his seat then started he,
And turned him round three times three.
The Moon at that sight blush'd scarlet red,
The stars threw down their cups & fled,
And all the devils that were in hell
Answered with a ninefold yell.
Klopstock felt the intripled turn,
And all his bowels began to churn,
And his bowels turned round three times three,
And lock'd in his soul with a ninefold key,
That from his body it ne'er could be parted
Till to the last trumpet it was farted.
Then again old Nobodaddy swore
He ne'er had seen such a thing before,
Since Noah was shut in the ark,
Since Eve first chose her hellfire spark,
Since 'twas the fashion to go naked,
Since the old anything was created,
And so feeling, he begg'd me to turn again
And ease poor Klopstock's ninefold pain.
If Blake could do this when he rose up from a shite,
What might he not do if he sat down to write?

A fairy leapt upon my knee
Singing & dancing merrily;
I said, "Thou thing of patches, rings,
Pins, Necklaces, & such like things,
Disguiser of the Female Form,
Thou paltry, gilded, poisonous worm!"
Weeping, he fell upon my thigh,
And thus in tears did soft reply:
"Knowest thou not, O Fairies' Lord!
How much by us Contemn'd, Abhorr'd,
Whatever hides the Female form
That cannot bear the Mental storm?
Therefore in Pity still we give
Our lives to make the Female live;
And what would turn into disease
We turn to what will joy & please."

My Specter around me night & day
Like a Wild beast guards my way.
My Emanation far within
Weeps incessantly for my Sin.

A Fathomless & boundless deep,
There we wander, there we weep;
On the hungry craving wind
My Specter follows thee behind.

He scents thy footsteps in the snow,
Wheresoever thou dost go
Thro' the wintry hail & rain.
When wilt thou return again?

Dost thou not in Pride & scorn
Fill with tempests all my morn,
And with jealousies & fears
Fill my pleasant nights with tears?

Seven of my sweet loves thy knife
Has bereaved of their life.
Their marble tombs I built with tears
And with cold & shuddering fears.

Seven more loves weep night & day
Round the tombs where my loves lay,
And seven more loves attend each night
Around my couch with torches bright.

And seven more Loves in my bed
Crown with wine my mournful head,
Pitying & forgiving all
Thy transgressions, great & small.

When wilt thou return & view
My loves, & them to life renew?
When wilt thou return & live?
When wilt thou pity as I forgive?

"Never, Never, I return:
Still for Victory I burn.
Living, thee alone I'll have
And when dead I'll be thy Grave.

"Thro' the Heaven & Earth & Hell
Thou shalt never never quell:
I will fly & thou pursue,
Night & Morn the flight renew."

Till I turn from Female Love,
And root up the Infernal Grove,
I shall never worthy be
To Step into Eternity.

And, to end thy cruel mocks,
Annihilate thee on the rocks,
And another form create
To be subservient to my Fate.

Let us agree to give up Love,
And root up the infernal grove;
Then shall we return & see
The worlds of happy Eternity.

& Throughout all Eternity
I forgive you, you forgive me.
As our dear Redeemer said:
"This the Wine & this the Bread."

[ADDITIONAL STANZAS]

O'er my Sins thou sit & moan:
Hast thou no sins of thy own?
O'er my Sins thou sit & weep,
And lull thy own Sins fast asleep.

What Transgressions I commit
Are for thy Transgressions fit.
They thy Harlots, thou their slave,
And my Bed becomes their Grave.

Poor pale pitiable form
That I follow in a Storm,
Iron tears & groans of lead
Bind around my aching head.

———◆◆◆———

When a Man has Married a Wife, he finds out whether
Her knees & elbows are only glued together.

Mock on, Mock on Voltaire, Rousseau:
Mock on, Mock on: 'tis all in vain!
You throw the sand against the wind,
And the wind blows it back again.

And every sand becomes a Gem
Reflected in the beams divine;
Blown back they blind the mocking Eye,
But still in Israel's paths they shine.

The Atoms of Democritus
And Newton's Particles of light
Are sands upon the Red Sea shore,
Where Israel's tents do shine so bright.

MORNING

To find the Western path
Right thro' the Gates of Wrath
I urge my way;
Sweet Mercy leads me on:
With soft repentant moan
I see the break of day.

The war of swords & spears
Melted by dewy tears
Exhales on high;
The Sun is freed from fears
And with soft grateful tears
Ascends the sky.

Each Man is in his Specter's power
Until the arrival of that hour,
When his Humanity awake
And cast his own Specter into the Lake.

THE BIRDS

He. Where thou dwellest, in what Grove,
    Tell me, Fair one, tell me, love;
    Where thou thy charming Nest dost build,
    O thou pride of every field!

She. Yonder stands a lonely tree,
    There I live & mourn for thee.
    Morning drinks my silent tear,
    And evening winds my sorrows bear.

He. O thou Summer's harmony,
    I have liv'd & mourn'd for thee.
    Each day I mourn along the wood,
    And night hath heard my sorrows loud.

She. Dost thou truly long for me?
    And am I thus sweet to thee?
    Sorrow now is at an End,
    O my Lover & my Friend!

He. Come, on wings of joy we'll fly
    To where my Bower hangs on high!
    Come, & make thy calm retreat
    Among green leaves & blossoms sweet!

TO THE QUEEN

The Door of Death is made of Gold,
That Mortal Eyes cannot behold;
But, when the Mortal Eyes are clos'd,
And cold and pale the Limbs repos'd,
The Soul awakes; and, wond'ring, sees
In her mild Hand the golden Keys:
The Grave is Heaven's golden Gate,
And rich and poor around it wait;
O Shepherdess of England's Fold,
Behold this Gate of Pearl and Gold!

To dedicate to England's Queen
The Visions that my Soul has seen,
And, by Her kind permission, bring
What I have borne on solemn Wing
From the vast regions of the Grave,
Before Her Throne my Wings I wave;
Bowing before my Sov'reign's Feet,
"The Grave produc'd these Blossoms sweet
In mild repose from Earthly strife;
The Blossoms of Eternal Life!"

The Angel that presided o'er my birth
Said, "Little creature, form'd of Joy & Mirth,
Go love without the help of any Thing on Earth."

Grown old in Love from Seven till Seven times Seven,
I oft have wish'd for Hell for Ease from Heaven.

Why was Cupid a Boy
And why a boy was he?
He should have been a Girl
For ought that I can see.

For he shoots with his bow,
And the Girl shoots with her Eye,
And they both are merry & glad
And laugh when we do cry.

And to make Cupid a Boy
Was the Cupid Girl's mocking plan;
For a boy can't interpret the thing
Till he is become a man.

And then he's so pierc'd with cares
And wounded with arrowy smarts,
That the whole business of his life
Is to pick out the heads of the darts.

'Twas the Greeks' love of war
Turn'd Love into a Boy,
And Woman into a Statue of Stone—
And away flew every Joy.

Since all the Riches of this World
May be gifts from the Devil & Earthly Kings,
I should suspect that I worshipp'd the Devil
If I thank'd my God for Worldly things.

Nail his neck to the Cross: nail it with a nail.
Nail his neck to the Cross: ye all have power over his tail.

The Caverns of the Grave I've seen,
And these I show'd to England's Queen.
But now the Caves of Hell I view:
Who shall I dare to show them to?
What mighty Soul in Beauty's form
Shall dauntless View the Infernal Storm?
Egremont's Countess can control
The flames of Hell that round me roll.
If she refuse, I still go on
Till the Heavens & Earth are gone,
Still admir'd by Noble minds,
Follow'd by Envy on the winds,
Re-engrav'd Time after Time,
Ever in their youthful prime,
My designs unchang'd remain.
Time may rage but rage in vain.
Far above Time's troubled Fountains
On the Great Atlantic Mountains,
In my Golden House on high,
There they Shine Eternally.

I rose up at the dawn of day—
Get thee away! get thee away!
Pray'st thou for Riches? away! away!
This is the Throne of Mammon gray.

Said I, "this sure is very odd.
I took it to be the Throne of God.
For every Thing besides I have:
It is only for Riches that I can crave.

"I have Mental Joy & Mental Health
And Mental Friends & Mental wealth;
I've a Wife I love & that loves me;
I've all but Riches Bodily.

"I am in God's presence night & day,
And he never turns his face away.
The accuser of sins by my side does stand
And he holds my money bag in his hand.

"For my worldly things God makes him pay,
And he'd pay more if to him I would pray;
And so you may do the worst you can do:
Be assur'd Mr. devil I won't pray to you.

"Then if for Riches I must not Pray,
God knows I little of Prayers need say.
So as a Church is known by its Steeple,
If I pray it must be for other People.

"He says, if I do not worship him for a God,
I shall eat coarser food & go worse shod;
So as I don't value such things as these,
You must do, Mr. devil, just as God please."

The Pickering
Manuscript

THE SMILE

There is a Smile of Love,
And there is a Smile of Deceit,
And there is a Smile of Smiles
In which these two Smiles meet.

And there is a Frown of Hate,
And there is a Frown of Disdain,
And there is a Frown of Frowns
Which you strive to forget in vain,

For it sticks in the Heart's deep Core
And it sticks in the deep Backbone;
And no Smile that ever was smil'd,
But only one Smile alone,

That betwixt the Cradle & Grave
It only once Smil'd can be;
But, when it once is Smil'd,
There's an end to all Misery.

THE GOLDEN NET

Three virgins at the break of day:
"Whither, young Man, whither away?
Alas for woe! alas for woe!"
They cry, & tears forever flow.
The one was Cloth'd in flames of fire,
The other Cloth'd in iron wire,
The other Cloth'd in tears & sighs
Dazzling bright before my Eyes.
They bore a Net of golden twine
To hang upon the branches fine.
Pitying I wept to see the woe
That Love & Beauty undergo,
To be consum'd in burning Fires
And in ungratified desires,
And in tears cloth'd Night & day
Melted all my Soul away.
When they saw my Tears, a Smile
That did Heaven itself beguile,
Bore the Golden Net aloft
As on downy Pinions soft
Over the Morning of my day.
Underneath the Net I stray,
Now entreating Burning Fire,
Now entreating Iron Wire,
Now entreating Tears & Sighs.
O when will the morning rise?

THE MENTAL TRAVELER

I travel'd thro' a Land of Men,
A Land of Men & Women too,
And heard & saw such dreadful things
As cold Earth wanderers never knew.

For there the Babe is born in joy
That was begotten in dire woe;
Just as we Reap in joy the fruit
Which we in bitter tears did sow.

And if the Babe is born a Boy
He's given to a Woman Old,
Who nails him down upon a rock,
Catches his shrieks in cups of gold.

She binds iron thorns around his head,
She pierces both his hands & feet,
She cuts his heart out at his side
To make it feel both cold & heat.

Her fingers number every Nerve,
Just as a Miser counts his gold;
She lives upon his shrieks & cries,
And she grows young as he grows old.

Till he becomes a bleeding youth,
And she becomes a Virgin bright;
Then he rends up his Manacles
And binds her down for his delight.

He plants himself in all her Nerves,
Just as a Husbandman his mold;
And she becomes his dwelling place
And Garden fruitful seventy fold.

An aged Shadow, soon he fades,
Wand'ring round an Earthly Cot,
Full filled all with gems & gold
Which he by industry had got.

And these are the gems of the Human Soul,
The rubies & pearls of a lovesick eye,
The countless gold of the aching heart,
The martyr's groan & the lover's sigh.

They are his meat, they are his drink;
He feeds the Beggar & the Poor
And the wayfaring Traveler:
Forever open is his door.

His grief is their eternal joy;
They make the roofs & walls to ring;
Till from the fire on the hearth
A little Female Babe does spring.

And she is all of solid fire
And gems & gold, that none his hand
Dares stretch to touch her Baby form,
Or wrap her in his swaddling-band.

But She comes to the Man she loves,
If young or old, or rich or poor;
They soon drive out the aged Host,
A Beggar at another's door.

He wanders weeping far away,
Until some other take him in;
Oft blind & age-bent, sore distressed,
Until he can a Maiden win.

And to allay his freezing Age
The Poor Man takes her in his arms;
The Cottage fades before his sight,
The Garden & its lovely Charms.

The Guests are scatter'd thro' the land,
For the Eye altering alters all;
The Senses roll themselves in fear,
And the flat Earth becomes a Ball;

The stars, sun, Moon, all shrink away,
A desert vast without a bound,
And nothing left to eat or drink,
And a dark desert all around.

The honey of her Infant lips,
The bread & wine of her sweet smile,
The wild game of her roving Eye,
Does him to Infancy beguile;

For as he eats & drinks he grows
Younger & younger every day;
And on the desert wild they both
Wander in terror & dismay.

Like the wild Stag she flees away,
Her fear plants many a thicket wild;
While he pursues her night & day,
By various arts of Love beguil'd,

By various arts of Love & Hate,
Till the wide desert planted o'er
With Labyrinths of wayward Love,
Where roam the Lion, Wolf & Boar,

Till he becomes a wayward Babe,
And she a weeping Woman Old.
Then many a Lover wanders here;
The Sun & Stars are nearer roll'd.

The trees bring forth sweet Ecstasy
To all who in the desert roam;
Till many a City there is Built,
And many a pleasant Shepherd's home.

But when they find the frowning Babe,
Terror strikes thro' the region wide:
They cry "The Babe! the Babe is Born!"
And flee away on Every side.

For who dare touch the frowning form,
His arm is wither'd to its root;
Lions, Boars, Wolves, all howling flee,
And every Tree does shed its fruit.

And none can touch that frowning form,
Except it be a Woman Old;
She nails him down upon the Rock,
And all is done as I have told.

THE LAND OF DREAMS

Awake, awake, my little Boy!
Thou wast thy Mother's only joy;
Why dost thou weep in thy gentle sleep?
Awake! thy Father does thee keep.

"O, what Land is the Land of Dreams?
What are its Mountains & what are its Streams?
O Father, I saw my Mother there,
Among the Lilies by waters fair.

"Among the Lambs, clothed in white,
She walk'd with her Thomas in sweet delight.
I wept for joy, like a dove I mourn;
O! when shall I again return?"

Dear Child, I also by pleasant Streams
Have wander'd all Night in the Land of Dreams;
But tho' calm & warm the waters wide,
I could not get to the other side.

"Father, O Father! what do we here
In this Land of unbelief & fear?
The Land of Dreams is better far,
Above the light of the Morning Star."

MARY

Sweet Mary, the first time she ever was there,
Came into the Ballroom among the Fair;
The young Men & Maidens around her throng,
And these are the words upon every tongue:

"An Angel is here from the heavenly climes,
Or again does return the golden times;
Her eyes outshine every brilliant ray,
She opens her lips—'tis the Month of May."

Mary moves in soft beauty & conscious delight
To augment with sweet smiles all the joys of the
    Night,
Nor once blushes to own to the rest of the Fair
That sweet Love & Beauty are worthy our care.

In the Morning the Villagers rose with delight
And repeated with pleasure the joys of the night,
And Mary arose among Friends to be free,
But no Friend from henceforward thou, Mary, shalt
    see.

Some said she was proud, some call'd her a whore,
And some, when she passed by, shut to the door;
A damp cold came o'er her, her blushes all fled;
Her lilies & roses are blighted & shed.

"O, why was I born with a different Face?
Why was I not born like this Envious Race?
Why did Heaven adorn me with bountiful hand,
And then set me down in an envious Land?

"To be weak as a Lamb & smooth as a dove,
And not to raise Envy, is call'd Christian Love;
But if you raise Envy your Merit's to blame
For planting such spite in the weak & the tame.

"I will humble my Beauty, I will not dress fine,
I will keep from the Ball, & my Eyes shall not shine;
And if any Girl's Lover forsakes her for me,
I'll refuse him my hand & from Envy be free."

She went out in Morning attir'd plain & neat;
"Proud Mary's gone Mad," said the Child in the
        Street:
She went out in Morning in plain neat attire,
And came home in Evening bespatter'd with mire.

She trembled & wept, sitting on the Bedside;
She forgot it was Night, & she trembled & cried;
She forgot it was Night, she forgot it was Morn,
Her soft Memory imprinted with Faces of Scorn,

With Faces of Scorn & with Eyes of disdain
Like foul Fiends inhabiting Mary's mild Brain;
She remembers no Face like the Human Divine.
All Faces have Envy, sweet Mary, but thine;

And thine is a Face of sweet Love in despair,
And thine is a Face of mild sorrow & care,
And thine is a Face of wild terror & fear
That shall never be quiet till laid on its bier.

THE CRYSTAL CABINET

The Maiden caught me in the Wild,
Where I was dancing merrily;
She put me into her Cabinet
And Lock'd me up with a golden Key.

This Cabinet is form'd of Gold
And Pearl & Crystal shining bright,
And within it opens into a World
And a little lovely Moony Night.

Another England there I saw,
Another London with its Tower,
Another Thames & other Hills,
And another pleasant Surrey Bower,

Another Maiden like herself,
Translucent, lovely, shining clear,
Threefold each in the other clos'd—
O, what a pleasant trembling fear!

O, what a smile! a threefold Smile
Fill'd me, that like a flame I burn'd;
I bent to Kiss the lovely Maid,
And found a Threefold Kiss return'd.

I strove to seize the inmost Form
With ardor fierce & hands of flame,
But burst the Crystal Cabinet,
And like a Weeping Babe became—

A weeping Babe upon the wild,
And Weeping Woman pale reclin'd,
And in the outward air again
I fill'd with woes the passing Wind.

THE GRAY MONK

"I die, I die!" the Mother said,
"My Children die for lack of Bread.
What more has the merciless Tyrant said?"
The Monk sat down on the Stony Bed.

The blood red ran from the Gray Monk's side,
His hands & feet were wounded wide,
His Body bent, his arms & knees
Like to the roots of ancient trees.

His eye was dry; no tear could flow:
A hollow groan first spoke his woe.
He trembled & shudder'd upon the Bed;
At length with a feeble cry he said:

"When God commanded this hand to write
In the studious hours of deep midnight,
He told me the writing I wrote should prove
The Bane of all that on Earth I lov'd.

"My Brother starv'd between two Walls,
His Children's Cry my Soul appalls;
I mock'd at the wrack & griding chain,
My bent body mocks their torturing pain.

"Thy Father drew his sword in the North,
With his thousands strong he marched forth;
Thy Brother has arm'd himself in Steel
To avenge the wrongs thy Children feel.

"But vain the Sword & vain the Bow,
They never can work War's overthrow.
The Hermit's Prayer & the Widow's tear
Alone can free the World from fear.

"For a Tear is an Intellectual Thing,
And a Sigh is the Sword of an Angel King,
And the bitter groan of the Martyr's woe
Is an Arrow from the Almighty's Bow.

"The hand of Vengeance found the Bed
To which the Purple Tyrant fled;
The iron hand crush'd the Tyrant's head
And became a Tyrant in his stead."

AUGURIES OF INNOCENCE

To see a World in a Grain of Sand
And a Heaven in a Wildflower,
Hold Infinity in the palm of your hand
And Eternity in an hour.

A Robin Redbreast in a Cage
Puts all Heaven in a Rage.
A dove house fill'd with doves & Pigeons
Shudders Hell thro' all its regions.
A dog starv'd at his Master's Gate
Predicts the ruin of the State.
A Horse misus'd upon the Road
Calls to Heaven for Human blood.
Each outcry of the hunted Hare
A fiber from the Brain does tear.
A Skylark wounded in the wing,
A Cherubim does cease to sing.
The Game Cock clipp'd & arm'd for fight
Does the Rising Sun affright.
Every Wolf's & Lion's howl
Raises from Hell a Human Soul.
The wild deer, wand'ring here & there,
Keeps the Human Soul from Care.
The Lamb misus'd breeds Public strife
And yet forgives the Butcher's Knife.
The Bat that flits at close of Eve
Has left the Brain that won't Believe.
The Owl that calls upon the Night
Speaks the Unbeliever's fright.
He who shall hurt the little Wren
Shall never be belov'd by Men.

He who the Ox to wrath has mov'd
Shall never be by Woman lov'd.
The wanton Boy that kills the Fly
Shall feel the Spider's enmity.
He who torments the Chafer's sprite
Weaves a Bower in endless Night.
The Caterpillar on the Leaf
Repeats to thee thy Mother's grief.
Kill not the Moth nor Butterfly,
For the Last Judgment draweth nigh.
He who shall train the Horse to War
Shall never pass the Polar Bar.
The Beggar's Dog & Widow's Cat,
Feed them & thou wilt grow fat.
The Gnat that sings his Summer's song
Poison gets from Slander's tongue.
The poison of the Snake & Newt
Is the sweat of Envy's Foot.
The Poison of the Honey Bee
Is the Artist's Jealousy.
The Prince's Robes & Beggar's Rags
Are Toadstools on the Miser's Bags.
A truth that's told with bad intent
Beats all the Lies you can invent.
It is right it should be so;
Man was made for Joy & Woe;
And when this we rightly know
Thro' the World we safely go.
Joy & Woe are woven fine,
A Clothing for the Soul divine;
Under every grief & pine
Runs a joy with silken twine.
The Babe is more than swaddling Bands;
Throughout all these Human Lands
Tools were made, & Born were hands,
Every Farmer Understands.

Every Tear from Every Eye
Becomes a Babe in Eternity;
This is caught by Females bright
And return'd to its own delight.
The Bleat, the Bark, Bellow & Roar
Are Waves that Beat on Heaven's Shore.
The Babe that weeps the Rod beneath
Writes Revenge in realms of death.
The Beggar's Rags, fluttering in Air,
Does to Rags the Heavens tear.
The Soldier, arm'd with Sword & Gun,
Palsied strikes the Summer's Sun.
The poor Man's Farthing is worth more
Than all the Gold on Afric's Shore.
One Mite wrung from the Lab'rer's hands
Shall buy & sell the Miser's Lands:
Or, if protected from on high,
Does that whole Nation sell & buy.
He who mocks the Infant's Faith
Shall be mock'd in Age & Death.
He who shall teach the Child to Doubt
The rotting Grave shall ne'er get out.
He who respects the Infant's faith
Triumphs over Hell & Death.
The Child's Toys & the Old Man's Reasons
Are the Fruits of the Two seasons.
The Questioner, who sits so sly,
Shall never know how to Reply.
He who replies to words of Doubt
Doth put the Light of Knowledge out.
The Strongest Poison ever known
Came from Caesar's Laurel Crown.
Naught can deform the Human Race
Like to the Armor's iron brace.
When Gold & Gems adorn the Plow
To peaceful Arts shall Envy Bow.

A Riddle or the Cricket's Cry
Is to Doubt a fit Reply.
The Emmet's Inch & Eagle's Mile
Make Lame Philosophy to smile.
He who Doubts from what he sees
Will ne'er Believe, do what you Please.
If the Sun & Moon should doubt,
They'd immediately Go out.
To be in a Passion you Good may do,
But no Good if a Passion is in you.
The Whore & Gambler, by the State
Licens'd, build that Nation's Fate.
The Harlot's cry from Street to Street
Shall weave Old England's winding Sheet.
The Winner's Shout, the Loser's Curse,
Dance before dead England's Hearse.
Every Night & every Morn
Some to Misery are Born.
Every Morn & every Night
Some are Born to sweet delight.
Some are Born to sweet delight,
Some are Born to Endless Night.
We are led to Believe a Lie
When we see not Thro' the Eye
Which was Born in a Night to perish in a Night
When the Soul Slept in Beams of Light.
God Appears & God is Light
To those poor Souls who dwell in Night,
But does a Human Form Display
To those who Dwell in Realms of day.

LONG JOHN BROWN &
LITTLE MARY BELL

Little Mary Bell had a Fairy in a Nut,
Long John Brown had the Devil in his Gut;
Long John Brown lov'd Little Mary Bell,
And the Fairy drew the Devil into the Nutshell.

Her Fairy Skipp'd out & her Fairy Skipp'd in;
He laugh'd at the Devil saying "Love is a Sin."
The Devil he raged & the Devil he was wroth,
And the Devil enter'd into the Young Man's broth.

He was soon in the Gut of the loving Young Swain,
For John eat & drank to drive away Love's pain;
But all he could do he grew thinner & thinner,
Tho' he eat & drank as much as ten Men for his dinner.

Some said he had a Wolf in his stomach day & night,
Some said he had the Devil & they guess'd right;
The Fairy skipp'd about in his Glory, Joy & Pride,
And he laugh'd at the Devil till poor John Brown died.

Then the Fairy skipp'd out of the old Nutshell,
And woe & alack for Pretty Mary Bell!
For the Devil crept in when the Fairy skipp'd out,
And there goes Miss Bell with her fusty old Nut.

WILLIAM BOND

I wonder whether the Girls are mad,
And I wonder whether they mean to kill,
And I wonder if William Bond will die,
For assuredly he is very ill.

He went to Church in a May morning
Attended by Fairies, one, two & three;
But the Angels of Providence drove them away,
And he return'd home in Misery.

He went not out to the Field nor Fold,
He went not out to the Village nor Town,
But he came home in a black, black cloud,
And took to his Bed & there lay down.

And an Angel of Providence at his Feet,
And an Angel of Providence at his Head,
And in the midst a Black, Black Cloud,
And in the midst the Sick Man on his Bed.

And on his Right hand was Mary Green,
And on his Left hand was his Sister Jane,
And their tears fell thro' the black, black Cloud
To drive away the sick man's pain.

"O William, if thou dost another Love,
Dost another Love better than poor Mary,
Go & take that other to be thy Wife,
And Mary Green shall her servant be."

"Yes, Mary, I do another Love,
Another I Love far better than thee,
And Another I will have for my Wife;
Then what have I to do with thee?

"For thou art Melancholy Pale,
And on thy Head is the cold Moon's shine,
But she is ruddy & bright as day,
And the sun beams dazzle from her eyne."

Mary trembled & Mary chill'd
And Mary fell down on the right hand floor,
That William Bond & his Sister Jane
Scarce could recover Mary more.

When Mary awoke & found her Laid
On the Right hand of her William dear,
On the Right hand of his loved Bed,
And saw her William Bond so near,

The Fairies that fled from William Bond
Danced around her Shining Head;
They danced over the Pillow white,
And the Angels of Providence left the Bed.

I thought Love liv'd in the hot sunshine,
But O, he lives in the Moony light!
I thought to find Love in the heat of day,
But sweet Love is the Comforter of Night.

Seek Love in the Pity of others' Woe,
In the gentle relief of another's care,
In the darkness of night & the winter's snow,
In the naked & outcast, Seek Love there!

Miscellaneous Works

THERE IS NO NATURAL RELIGION

[a]

The Argument. Man has no notion of moral fitness but from Education. Naturally he is only a natural organ subject to Sense.

I. Man cannot naturally Perceive but through his natural or bodily organs.

II. Man by his reasoning power can only compare & judge of what he has already perceiv'd.

III. From a perception of only 3 senses or 3 elements none could deduce a fourth or fifth.

IV. None could have other than natural or organic thoughts if he had none but organic perceptions.

V. Man's desires are limited by his perceptions, none can desire what he has not perceiv'd.

VI. The desires & perceptions of man, untaught by anything but organs of sense, must be limited to objects of sense.

Conclusion. If it were not for the Poetic or Prophetic character, the Philosophic & Experimental would soon be at the ratio of all things, & stand still, unable to do other than repeat the same dull round over again.

THERE IS NO NATURAL RELIGION

[b]

I. Man's perceptions are not bounded by organs of perception; he perceives more than sense (tho' ever so acute) can discover.

II. Reason, or the ratio of all we have already known, is not the same that it shall be when we know more.

III. [Lost]

IV. The bounded is loathed by its possessor. The same dull round, even of a universe, would soon become a mill with complicated wheels.

V. If the many become the same as the few when possess'd, More! More! is the cry of a mistaken soul; less than All cannot satisfy Man.

VI. If any could desire what he is incapable of possessing, despair must be his eternal lot.

VII. The desire of Man being Infinite, the possession is Infinite & himself Infinite.

Application. He who sees the Infinite in all things, sees God. He who sees the Ratio only, sees himself only.
Therefore God becomes as we are, that we may be as he is.

ALL RELIGIONS ARE ONE

THE VOICE OF ONE CRYING IN THE WILDERNESS

The Argument. As the true method of knowledge is experiment, the true faculty of knowing must be the faculty which experiences. This faculty I treat of.

PRINCIPLE 1ST. That the Poetic Genius is the true Man, and that the body or outward form of Man is derived from the Poetic Genius. Likewise that the forms of all things are derived from their Genius, which by the Ancients was call'd an Angel & Spirit & Demon.

PRINCIPLE 2D. As all men are alike in outward form, So (and with the same infinite variety) all are alike in the Poetic Genius.

PRINCIPLE 3D. No man can think, write, or speak from his heart, but he must intend truth. Thus all sects of Philosophy are from the Poetic Genius adapted to the weaknesses of every individual.

PRINCIPLE 4TH. As none by traveling over known lands can find out the unknown, So from already acquired knowledge Man could not acquire more: therefore an universal Poetic Genius exists.

PRINCIPLE 5TH. The Religions of all Nations are derived from each Nation's different reception of the Poetic Genius, which is everywhere call'd the Spirit of Prophecy.

PRINCIPLE 6TH. The Jewish & Christian Testaments are an original derivation from the Poetic Genius; this is necessary from the confined nature of bodily sensation.

PRINCIPLE 7TH. As all men are alike (tho' infinitely various), So all Religions &, as all similars, have one source.

The true Man is the source, he being the Poetic Genius.

The Book
of Thel

THE BOOK OF THEL

Does the Eagle know what is in the pit?
Or wilt thou go ask the Mole?
Can Wisdom be put in a silver rod?
Or Love in a golden bowl?

I

The daughters of the Seraphim led round their sunny flocks,
All but the youngest: she in paleness sought the secret air,
To fade away like morning beauty from her mortal day:
Down by the river of Adona her soft voice is heard,
And thus her gentle lamentation falls like morning dew:

"O life of this our spring! why fades the lotus of the water,
Why fade these children of the spring, born but to smile &
    fall?
Ah! Thel is like a wat'ry bow, and like a parting cloud;
Like a reflection in a glass; like shadows in the water;
Like dreams of infants, like a smile upon an infant's face;
Like the dove's voice; like transient day; like music in the air.
Ah! gentle may I lay me down, and gentle rest my head,
And gentle sleep the sleep of death, and gentle hear the voice
Of him that walketh in the garden in the evening time."

The Lily of the Valley, breathing in the humble grass,
Answer'd the lovely maid and said: "I am a wat'ry weed,
And I am very small and love to dwell in lowly vales;
So weak, the gilded butterfly scarce perches on my head.
Yet I am visited from heaven, and he that smiles on all
Walks in the valley and each morn over me spreads his hand,
Saying, 'Rejoice, thou humble grass, thou newborn lily flower,
Thou gentle maid of silent valleys and of modest brooks;

For thou shalt be clothed in light, and fed with morning
    manna,
Till summer's heat melts thee beside the fountains and the
    springs
To flourish in eternal vales.' Then why should Thel complain?
Why should the mistress of the vales of Har utter a sigh?"

She ceas'd & smil'd in tears, then sat down in her silver
    shrine.

Thel answer'd: "O thou little virgin of the peaceful valley,
Giving to those that cannot crave, the voiceless, the o'ertired;
Thy breath doth nourish the innocent lamb, he smells thy
    milky garments,
He crops thy flowers while thou sittest smiling in his face,
Wiping his mild and meekin mouth from all contagious taints.
Thy wine doth purify the golden honey; thy perfume,
Which thou dost scatter on every little blade of grass that
    springs,
Revives the milked cow, & tames the fire-breathing steed.
But Thel is like a faint cloud kindled at the rising sun:
I vanish from my pearly throne, and who shall find my place?"

"Queen of the vales," the Lily answer'd, "ask the tender cloud,
And it shall tell thee why it glitters in the morning sky,
And why it scatters its bright beauty thro' the humid air.
Descend, O little Cloud, & hover before the eyes of Thel."
The Cloud descended, and the Lily bow'd her modest head
And went to mind her numerous charge among the verdant
    grass.

II

"O little Cloud," the virgin said, "I charge thee tell to me
Why thou complainest not when in one hour thou fade away:
Then we shall seek thee, but not find. Ah! Thel is like to thee:
I pass away: yet I complain, and no one hears my voice."

The Cloud then show'd his golden head & his bright form
    emerg'd,
Hovering and glittering on the air before the face of Thel.

"O virgin, know'st thou not our steeds drink of the golden
    springs
Where Luvah doth renew his horses? Look'st thou on my
    youth,
And fearest thou, because I vanish and am seen no more,
Nothing remains? O maid, I tell thee, when I pass away
It is to tenfold life, to love, to peace and raptures holy:
Unseen descending, weigh my light wings upon balmy flowers,
And court the fair-eyed dew to take me to her shining tent:
The weeping virgin, trembling kneels before the risen sun,
Till we arise link'd in a golden band and never part,
But walk united, bearing food to all our tender flowers."

"Dost thou, O little Cloud? I fear that I am not like thee,
For I walk thro' the vales of Har, and smell the sweetest
    flowers,
But I feed not the little flowers; I hear the warbling birds,
But I feed not the warbling birds; they fly and seek their food:
But Thel delights in these no more, because I fade away;
And all shall say, 'Without a use this shining woman liv'd,
Or did she only live to be at death the food of worms?'"

The Cloud reclin'd upon his airy throne and answer'd thus:

"Then if thou art the food of worms, O virgin of the skies,
How great thy use, how great thy blessing! Everything that
    lives
Lives not alone nor for itself. Fear not, and I will call
The weak worm from its lowly bed, and thou shalt hear its
    voice.
Come forth, worm of the silent valley, to thy pensive queen."

The helpless worm arose, and sat upon the Lily's leaf,
And the bright Cloud sail'd on, to find his partner in the vale.

III

Then Thel astonish'd view'd the Worm upon its dewy bed.

"Art thou a Worm? Image of weakness, art thou but a Worm?
I see thee like an infant wrapped in the Lily's leaf.
Ah! weep not, little voice, thou canst not speak, but thou
  canst weep.
Is this a Worm? I see thee lay helpless & naked, weeping,
And none to answer, none to cherish thee with mother's
  smiles."

The Clod of Clay heard the Worm's voice & rais'd her pitying
  head:
She bow'd over the weeping infant, and her life exhal'd
In milky fondness: then on Thel she fix'd her humble eyes.

"O beauty of the vales of Har! we live not for ourselves.
Thou seest me the meanest thing, and so I am indeed.
My bosom of itself is cold, and of itself is dark;
But he, that loves the lowly, pours his oil upon my head,
And kisses me, and binds his nuptial bands around my breast,
And says: 'Thou mother of my children, I have loved thee
And I have given thee a crown that none can take away.'
But how this is, sweet maid, I know not, and I cannot know;
I ponder, and I cannot ponder; yet I live and love."

The daughter of beauty wip'd her pitying tears with her white
  veil,
And said: "Alas! I knew not this, and therefore did I weep.
That God would love a Worm I knew, and punish the evil foot
That willful bruis'd its helpless form; but that he cherish'd it
With milk and oil I never knew, and therefore did I weep;
And I complain'd in the mild air, because I fade away,

And lay me down in thy cold bed, and leave my shining lot."
"Queen of the vales," the matron Clay answer'd, "I heard thy
    sighs,
And all thy moans flew o'er my roof, but I have call'd them
    down.
Wilt thou, O Queen, enter my house? 'Tis given thee to enter
And to return: fear nothing, enter with thy virgin feet."

IV

The eternal gates' terrific porter lifted the northern bar:
Thel enter'd in & saw the secrets of the land unknown.
She saw the couches of the dead, & where the fibrous roots
Of every heart on earth infixes deep its restless twists:
A land of sorrows & of tears where never smile was seen.

She wander'd in the land of clouds thro' valleys dark, list'ning
Dolors & lamentations; waiting oft beside a dewy grave
She stood in silence, list'ning to the voices of the ground,
Till to her own grave plot she came, & there she sat down,
And heard this voice of sorrow breathed from the hollow pit.

"Why cannot the Ear be closed to its own destruction?
Or the glist'ning Eye to the poison of a smile?
Why are Eyelids stor'd with arrows ready drawn,
Where a thousand fighting men in ambush lie?
Or an Eye of gifts & graces show'ring fruits & coined gold?
Why a Tongue impress'd with honey from every wind?
Why an Ear, a whirlpool fierce to draw creations in?
Why a Nostril wide inhaling terror, trembling, & affright?
Why a tender curb upon the youthful burning boy?
Why a little curtain of flesh on the bed of our desire?"

The Virgin started from her seat, & with a shriek
Fled back unhinder'd till she came into the vales of Har.

THE END

Visions of the Daughters of Albion

VISIONS OF THE DAUGHTERS
OF ALBION

The Eye sees more than the Heart knows

THE ARGUMENT

I loved Theotormon,
And I was not ashamed;
I trembled in my virgin fears,
And I hid in Leutha's vale!

I plucked Leutha's flower,
And I rose up from the vale;
But the terrible thunders tore
My virgin mantle in twain.

VISIONS

Enslav'd, the Daughters of Albion weep; a trembling
    lamentation
Upon their mountains; in their valleys, sighs toward America.

For the soft soul of America, Oothoon, wander'd in woe,
Along the vales of Leutha seeking flowers to comfort her;
And thus she spoke to the bright Marigold of Leutha's vale:

"Art thou a flower? art thou a nymph? I see thee now a
    flower,
Now a nymph! I dare not pluck thee from thy dewy bed!"

The Golden nymph replied: "Pluck thou my flower, Oothoon
    the mild!
Another flower shall spring, because the soul of sweet delight
Can never pass away." She ceas'd, & clos'd her golden shrine.

Then Oothoon pluck'd the flower, saying: "I pluck thee from thy bed,
Sweet flower, and put thee here to glow between my breasts,
And thus I turn my face to where my whole soul seeks."

Over the waves she went in wing'd exulting swift delight,
And over Theotormon's reign took her impetuous course.

Bromion rent her with his thunders; on his stormy bed
Lay the faint maid, and soon her woes appall'd his thunders hoarse.

Bromion spoke: "Behold this harlot here on Bromion's bed,
And let the jealous dolphins sport around the lovely maid!
Thy soft American plains are mine, and mine thy north & south:
Stamped with my signet are the swarthy children of the sun;
They are obedient, they resist not, they obey the scourge;
Their daughters worship terrors and obey the violent.
Now thou mayest marry Bromion's harlot, and protect the child
Of Bromion's rage, that Oothoon shall put forth in nine moons' time."

Then storms rent Theotormon's limbs: he rolled his waves around
And folded his black jealous waters round the adulterate pair.
Bound back to back in Bromion's caves, terror & meekness dwell:

At entrance Theotormon sits, wearing the threshold hard
With secret tears; beneath him sound like waves on a desert shore
The voice of slaves beneath the sun, and children bought with money,
That shiver in religious caves beneath the burning fires

Of lust, that belch incessant from the summits of the earth.
Oothoon weeps not; she cannot weep! her tears are locked up;
But she can howl incessant writhing her soft snowy limbs
And calling Theotormon's Eagles to prey upon her flesh.

"I call with holy voice! Kings of the sounding air,
Rend away this defiled bosom that I may reflect
The image of Theotormon on my pure transparent breast."

The Eagles at her call descend & rend their bleeding prey:
Theotormon severely smiles; her soul reflects the smile,
As the clear spring, mudded with feet of beasts, grows pure
    & smiles.

The Daughters of Albion hear her woes, & echo back her
    sighs.

"Why does my Theotormon sit weeping upon the threshold,
And Oothoon hovers by his side, persuading him in vain?
I cry: arise, O Theotormon! for the village dog
Barks at the breaking day; the nightingale has done lamenting;
The lark does rustle in the ripe corn, and the Eagle returns
From nightly prey and lifts his golden beak to the pure east,
Shaking the dust from his immortal pinions to awake
The sun that sleeps too long. Arise, my Theotormon, I am pure
Because the night is gone that clos'd me in its deadly black.
They told me that the night & day were all that I could see;
They told me that I had five senses to enclose me up,
And they enclos'd my infinite brain into a narrow circle,
And sunk my heart into the Abyss, a red, round globe, hot
    burning,
Till all from life I was obliterated and erased.
Instead of morn arises a bright shadow, like an eye
In the eastern cloud; instead of night a sickly charnel house:
That Theotormon hears me not! to him the night and morn

Are both alike; a night of sighs, a morning of fresh tears,
And none but Bromion can hear my lamentations.
"With what sense is it that the chicken shuns the ravenous
  hawk?
With what sense does the tame pigeon measure out the
  expanse?
With what sense does the bee form cells? have not the mouse
  & frog
Eyes and ears and sense of touch? yet are their habitations
And their pursuits as different as their forms and as their joys.
Ask the wild ass why he refuses burdens, and the meek camel
Why he loves man: is it because of eye, ear, mouth, or skin,
Or breathing nostrils? No, for these the wolf and tyger have.
Ask the blind worm the secrets of the grave, and why her
  spires
Love to curl round the bones of death; and ask the rav'nous
  snake
Where she gets poison, & the wing'd eagle why he loves the
  sun;
And then tell me the thoughts of man, that have been hid of
  old.

"Silent I hover all the night, and all day could be silent
If Theotormon once would turn his loved eyes upon me.
How can I be defil'd when I reflect thy image pure?
Sweetest the fruit that the worm feeds on, & the soul prey'd
  on by woe,
The new wash'd lamb ting'd with the village smoke, & the
  bright swan
By the red earth of our immortal river. I bathe my wings,
And I am white and pure to hover round Theotormon's breast."

Then Theotormon broke his silence, and he answered:
"Tell me what is the night or day to one o'erflow'd with woe?
Tell me what is a thought, & of what substance is it made?

Tell me what is a joy, & in what gardens do joys grow?
And in what rivers swim the sorrows? and upon what
    mountains

Wave shadows of discontent? and in what houses dwell the
    wretched,
Drunken with woe forgotten, and shut up from cold despair?

"Tell me where dwell the thoughts forgotten till thou call
    them forth?
Tell me where dwell the joys of old? & where the ancient
    loves,
And when will they renew again, & the night of oblivion past,
That I might traverse times & spaces far remote, and bring
Comforts into a present sorrow and a night of pain?
Where goest thou, O thought? to what remote land is thy
    flight?
If thou returnest to the present moment of affliction
Wilt thou bring comforts on thy wings, and dews and honey
    and balm,
Or poison from the desert wilds, from the eyes of the envier?"

Then Bromion said, and shook the cavern with his
    lamentation:
"Thou knowest that the ancient trees seen by thine eyes have
    fruit,
But knowest thou that trees and fruits flourish upon the earth
To gratify senses unknown? trees, beasts and birds unknown;
Unknown, not unperceiv'd, spread in the infinite microscope,
In places yet unvisited by the voyager, and in worlds
Over another kind of seas, and in atmospheres unknown:
Ah! are there other wars beside the wars of sword and fire?
And are there other sorrows beside the sorrows of poverty?
And are there other joys beside the joys of riches and ease?
And is there not one law for both the lion and the ox?

And is there not eternal fire and eternal chains
To bind the phantoms of existence from eternal life?"

Then Oothoon waited silent all the day and all the night;
But when the morn arose, her lamentation renew'd.
The Daughters of Albion hear her woes, & echo back her
     sighs.

"O Urizen! Creator of men! mistaken Demon of heaven!
Thy joys are tears, thy labor vain to form men to thine image.
How can one joy absorb another? are not different joys
Holy, eternal, infinite? and each joy is a Love.

"Does not the great mouth laugh at a gift, & the narrow
     eyelids mock
At the labor that is above payment? and wilt thou take the ape
For thy counsellor, or the dog for a schoolmaster to thy
     children?
Does he who contemns poverty and he who turns with
     abhorrence
From usury feel the same passion, or are they moved alike?
How can the giver of gifts experience the delights of the
     merchant?
How the industrious citizen the pains of the husbandman?
How different far the fat fed hireling with hollow drum,
Who buys whole corn fields into wastes, and sings upon the
     heath!
How different their eye and ear! how different the world to
     them!
With what sense does the parson claim the labor of the
     farmer?
What are his nets & gins & traps; & how does he surround him
With cold floods of abstraction, and with forests of solitude,
To build him castles and high spires, where kings & priests
     may dwell;

Till she who burns with youth, and knows no fixed lot, is
    bound
In spells of law to one she loathes? and must she drag the
    chain
Of life in weary lust? must chilling, murderous thoughts
    obscure
The clear heaven of her eternal spring; to bear the wintry rage
Of a harsh terror, driv'n to madness, bound to hold a rod
Over her shrinking shoulders all the day, & all the night
To turn the wheel of false desire, and longings that wake her
    womb
To the abhorred birth of cherubs in the human form,
That live a pestilence & die a meteor, & are no more;
Till the child dwell with one he hates, and do the deed he
    loathes,
And the impure scourge force his seed into its unripe birth
Ere yet his eyelids can behold the arrows of the day?

"Does the whale worship at thy footsteps as the hungry dog;
Or does he scent the mountain prey because his nostrils wide
Draw in the ocean? does his eye discern the flying cloud
As the raven's eye? or does he measure the expanse like the
    vulture?
Does the still spider view the cliffs where eagles hide their
    young;
Or does the fly rejoice because the harvest is brought in?
Does not the eagle scorn the earth & despise the treasures
    beneath?
But the mole knoweth what is there, & the worm shall tell it
    thee.
Does not the worm erect a pillar in the moldering churchyard
And a palace of eternity in the jaws of the hungry grave?
Over his porch these words are written: 'Take thy bliss, O
    Man!
And sweet shall be thy taste, & sweet thy infant joys renew!'

"Infancy! fearless, lustful, happy, nestling for delight
In laps of pleasure: Innocence! honest, open, seeking
The vigorous joys of morning light; open to virgin bliss.
Who taught thee modesty, subtle modesty, child of night &
      sleep?
When thou awakest wilt thou dissemble all thy secret joys,
Or wert thou not awake when all this mystery was disclos'd?
Then com'st thou forth a modest virgin, knowing to dissemble,
With nets found under thy night pillow, to catch virgin joy
And brand it with the name of whore, & sell it in the night,
In silence, ev'n without a whisper, and in seeming sleep.
Religious dreams and holy vespers light thy smoky fires:
Once were thy fires lighted by the eyes of honest morn.
And does my Theotormon seek this hypocrite modesty,
This knowing, artful, secret, fearful, cautious, trembling
      hypocrite?
Then is Oothoon a whore indeed! and all the virgin joys
Of life are harlots, and Theotormon is a sick man's dream;
And Oothoon is the crafty slave of selfish holiness.

"But Oothoon is not so: a virgin fill'd with virgin fancies,
Open to joy and to delight where ever beauty appears;
If in the morning sun I find it, there my eyes are fix'd
In happy copulation; if in evening mild, wearied with work,
Sit on a bank and draw the pleasures of this free born joy.

"The moment of desire! the moment of desire! The virgin
That pines for man shall awaken her womb to enormous joys
In the secret shadows of her chamber: the youth shut up from
The lustful joy shall forget to generate & create an amorous
      image
In the shadows of his curtains and in the folds of his silent
      pillow.
Are not these the places of religion, the rewards of continence,
The self enjoyings of self denial? why dost thou seek religion?

Is it because acts are not lovely that thou seekest solitude
Where the horrible darkness is impressed with reflections of
     desire?

"Father of Jealousy, be thou accursed from the earth!
Why hast thou taught my Theotormon this accursed thing?
Till beauty fades from off my shoulders, darken'd and cast out,
A solitary shadow wailing on the margin of nonentity.

"I cry: Love! Love! Love! happy happy Love! free as the
     mountain wind!
Can that be Love that drinks another as a sponge drinks
     water,
That clouds with jealousy his nights, with weepings all the day,
To spin a web of age around him, gray and hoary, dark,
Till his eyes sicken at the fruit that hangs before his sight?
Such is self-love that envies all, a creeping skeleton
With lamplike eyes watching around the frozen marriage bed.

"But silken nets and traps of adamant will Oothoon spread,
And catch for thee girls of mild silver, or of furious gold.
I'll lie beside thee on a bank & view their wanton play
In lovely copulation, bliss on bliss, with Theotormon:
Red as the rosy morning, lustful as the firstborn beam,
Oothoon shall view his dear delight, nor e'er with jealous cloud
Come in the heaven of generous love, nor selfish blightings
     bring.

"Does the sun walk in glorious raiment on the secret floor
Where the cold miser spreads his gold; or does the bright
     cloud drop
On his stone threshold? does his eye behold the beam that
     brings
Expansion to the eye of pity? or will he bind himself
Beside the ox to thy hard furrow? does not that mild beam blot

The bat, the owl, the glowing tyger, and the king of night?
The sea fowl takes the wintry blast for a cov'ring to her limbs,
And the wild snake the pestilence to adorn him with gems &
 gold;
And trees & birds & beasts & men behold their eternal joy.
Arise, you little glancing wings, and sing your infant joy!
Arise, and drink your bliss, for everything that lives is holy!"

Thus every morning wails Oothoon; but Theotormon sits
Upon the margin'd ocean conversing with shadows dire.
The Daughters of Albion hear her woes, & echo back her
 sighs.

THE END

The Marriage of Heaven and Hell

THE MARRIAGE OF HEAVEN AND HELL

THE ARGUMENT

Rintrah roars & shakes his fires in the burdened air;
Hungry clouds swag on the deep.

Once meek, and in a perilous path,
The just man kept his course along
The vale of death.
Roses are planted where thorns grow.
And on the barren heath
Sing the honeybees.

Then the perilous path was planted:
And a river, and a spring
On every cliff and tomb;
And on the bleached bones
Red clay brought forth.

Till the villain left the paths of ease,
To walk in perilous paths, and drive
The just man into barren climes.

Now the sneaking serpent walks
In mild humility.
And the just man rages in the wilds
Where lions roam.

Rintrah roars & shakes his fires in the burdened air;
Hungry clouds swag on the deep.

As a new heaven is begun, and it is now thirty-three years since its advent: the Eternal Hell revives. And lo! Swedenborg is the Angel sitting at the tomb; his writings are the linen clothes folded up. Now is the dominion of Edom, & the return of Adam into Paradise; see Isaiah xxxiv & xxxv Chap:

Without Contraries is no progression. Attraction and Repulsion, Reason and Energy, Love and Hate, are necessary to Human existence.

From these contraries spring what the religious call Good & Evil. Good is the passive that obeys Reason. Evil is the active springing from Energy.

Good is Heaven. Evil is Hell.

THE VOICE OF THE DEVIL

All Bibles or sacred codes have been the causes of the following Errors:

1. That Man has two real existing principles Viz: a Body & a Soul.

2. That Energy, called Evil, is alone from the Body, & that Reason, called Good, is alone from the Soul.

3. That God will torment Man in Eternity for following his Energies.

But the following Contraries to these are True:

1. Man has no Body distinct from his Soul; for that called Body is a portion of Soul discerned by the five Senses, the chief inlets of Soul in this age.

2. Energy is the only life and is from the Body and Reason is the bound or outward circumference of Energy.

3. Energy is Eternal Delight.

Those who restrain desire, do so because theirs is weak enough to be restrained; and the restrainer or reason usurps its place & governs the unwilling.

And being restrained it by degrees becomes passive till it is only the shadow of desire.

The history of this is written in Paradise Lost & the Governor or Reason is call'd Messiah.

And the original Archangel or possessor of the command of the heavenly host, is called the Devil or Satan and his children are call'd Sin & Death.

But in the Book of Job, Milton's Messiah is call'd Satan.

For this history has been adopted by both parties.

It indeed appear'd to Reason as if Desire was cast out, but the Devil's account is, that the Messiah fell, & formed a heaven of what he stole from the Abyss.

This is shown in the Gospel, where he prays to the Father to send the comforter or Desire that Reason may have Ideas to build on, the Jehovah of the Bible being no other than he, who dwells in flaming fire.

Know that after Christ's death, he became Jehovah.

But in Milton; the Father is Destiny, the Son, a Ratio of the five senses & the Holy Ghost, Vacuum!

Note. The reason Milton wrote in fetters when he wrote of Angels & God, and at liberty when of Devils & Hell, is because he was a true Poet and of the Devil's party without knowing it.

A MEMORABLE FANCY.

As I was walking among the fires of hell, delighted with the enjoyments of Genius, which to Angels look like torment and insanity, I collected some of their Proverbs; thinking that as the sayings used in a nation, mark its character, so the Proverbs of Hell show the nature of Infernal wisdom better than any description of buildings or garments.

When I came home, on the abyss of the five senses, where a flat sided steep frowns over the present world, I saw a mighty Devil folded in black clouds, hovering on the sides of the rock: with corroding fires he wrote the following sentence now perceived by the minds of men, & read by them on earth:

How do you know but ev'ry Bird that cuts the airy way,
Is an immense world of delight, clos'd by your senses five?

Proverbs of Hell

1. In seed time learn, in harvest teach, in winter enjoy.
2. Drive your cart and your plow over the bones of the dead.
3. The road of excess leads to the palace of wisdom.
4. Prudence is a rich ugly old maid courted by Incapacity.
5. He who desires but acts not, breeds pestilence.
6. The cut worm forgives the plow.
7. Dip him in the river who loves water.
8. A fool sees not the same tree that a wise man sees.
9. He whose face gives no light, shall never become a star.
10. Eternity is in love with the productions of time.
11. The busy bee has no time for sorrow.
12. The hours of folly are measur'd by the clock, but of wisdom, no clock can measure.
13. All wholesome food is caught without a net or a trap.
14. Bring out number, weight & measure in a year of dearth.
15. No bird soars too high, if he soars with his own wings.
16. A dead body revenges not injuries.
17. The most sublime act is to set another before you.
18. If the fool would persist in his folly he would become wise.
19. Folly is the cloak of knavery.
20. Shame is Pride's cloak.
21. Prisons are built with stones of Law, Brothels with bricks of Religion.
22. The pride of the peacock is the glory of God.
23. The lust of the goat is the bounty of God.
24. The wrath of the lion is the wisdom of God.
25. The nakedness of woman is the work of God.
26. Excess of sorrow laughs. Excess of joy weeps.
27. The roaring of lions, the howling of wolves, the raging of the stormy sea, and the destructive sword, are portions of eternity too great for the eye of man.

28. The fox condemns the trap, not himself.
29. Joys impregnate. Sorrows bring forth.
30. Let man wear the fell of the lion, woman the fleece of the sheep.
31. The bird a nest, the spider a web, man friendship.
32. The selfish, smiling fool & the sullen, frowning fool shall be both thought wise, that they may be a rod.
33. What is now proved was once only imagin'd.
34. The rat, the mouse, the fox, the rabbit watch the roots; the lion, the tyger, the horse, the elephant, watch the fruits.
35. The cistern contains: the fountain overflows.
36. One thought fills immensity.
37. Always be ready to speak your mind, and a base man will avoid you.
38. Everything possible to be believ'd is an image of truth.
39. The eagle never lost so much time as when he submitted to learn of the crow.
40. The fox provides for himself, but God provides for the lion.
41. Think in the morning, Act in the noon, Eat in the evening, Sleep in the night.
42. He who has suffered you to impose on him knows you.
43. As the plow follows words, so God rewards prayers.
44. The tygers of wrath are wiser than the horses of instruction
45. Expect poison from the standing water.
46. You never know what is enough unless you know what is more than enough.
47. Listen to the fools reproach! it is a kingly title!
48. The eyes of fire, the nostrils of air, the mouth of water, the beard of earth.
49. The weak in courage is strong in cunning.
50. The apple tree never asks the beech how he shall grow, nor the lion the horse, how he shall take his prey.
51. The thankful receiver bears a plentiful harvest.
52. If others had not been foolish, we should be so.
53. The soul of sweet delight can never be defil'd,

54. When thou seest an Eagle, thou seest a portion of Genius, lift up thy head!
55. As the caterpillar chooses the fairest leaves to lay her eggs on, so the priest lays his curse on the fairest joys.
56. To create a little flower is the labor of ages.
57. Damn braces: Bless relaxes.
58. The best wine is the oldest, the best water the newest.
59. Prayers plow not! Praises reap not!
60. Joys laugh not! Sorrows weep not!
61. The head Sublime, the heart Pathos, the genitals Beauty, the hands & feet Proportion.
62. As the air to a bird or the sea to a fish, so is contempt to the contemptible.
63. The crow wish'd everything was black, the owl, that everything was white.
64. Exuberance is Beauty.
65. If the lion was advised by the fox, he would be cunning.
66. Improvement makes straight roads, but the crooked roads without Improvement are roads of Genius.
67. Sooner murder an infant in its cradle than nurse unacted desires.
68. Where man is not nature is barren.
69. Truth can never be told so as to be understood, and not be believ'd.
70. Enough! or Too much.

The ancient Poets animated all sensible objects with Gods or Geniuses, calling them by the names and adorning them with the properties of woods, rivers, mountains, lakes, cities, nations, and whatever their enlarged & numerous senses could perceive.

And particularly they studied the genius of each city & country, placing it under its mental deity.

Till a system was formed, which some took advantage of & enslav'd the vulgar by attempting to realize or abstract the mental deities from their objects: thus began Priesthood.

Choosing forms of worship from poetic tales.

And at length they pronounced that the Gods had ordered such things.

Thus men forgot that All deities reside in the human breast.

A Memorable Fancy

The Prophets Isaiah and Ezekiel dined with me, and I asked them how they dared so roundly to assert that God spake to them; and whether they did not think at the time that they would be misunderstood, & so be the cause of imposition.

Isaiah answer'd, "I saw no God nor heard any, in a finite organical perception; but my senses discover'd the infinite in everything, and as I was then persuaded, & remain confirm'd, that the voice of honest indignation is the voice of God, I cared not for consequences but wrote."

Then I asked: "Does a firm persuasion that a thing is so, make it so?"

He replied, "All poets believe that it does, & in ages of imagination this firm persuasion removed mountains; but many are not capable of a firm persuasion of anything."

Then Ezekiel said, "The philosophy of the East taught the first principles of human perception. Some nations held one principle for the origin & some another, we of Israel taught that the Poetic Genius (as you now call it) was the first principle and all the others merely derivative, which was the cause of our despising the Priests & Philosophers of other countries, and prophesying that all Gods would at last be proved to originate in ours & to be the tributaries of the Poetic Genius; it was this that our great poet King David desired so fervently & invokes so pathetically, saying by this he conquers enemies & governs kingdoms; and we so loved our God, that we cursed in his name all the deities of surrounding nations, and asserted that they had rebelled; from these opinions the vulgar came to think that all nations would at last be subject to the Jews.

"This," said he, "like all firm persuasions, is come to pass, for all nations believe the Jews' code and worship the Jews' god, and what greater subjection can be?"

I heard this with some wonder, & must confess my own conviction. After dinner I ask'd Isaiah to favor the world with his lost works; he said none of equal value was lost. Ezekiel said the same of his.

I also asked Isaiah what made him go naked and barefoot three years? He answered, "The same that made our friend Diogenes the Grecian."

I then asked Ezekiel why he eat dung, & lay so long on his right & left side? He answered, "The desire of raising other men into a perception of the infinite: this the North American tribes practice, & is he honest who resists his genius or conscience only for the sake of present ease or gratification?"

The ancient tradition that the world will be consumed in fire at the end of six thousand years is true, as I have heard from Hell.

For the cherub with his flaming sword is hereby commanded to leave his guard at the tree of life, and when he does, the whole creation will be consumed, and appear infinite and holy, whereas it now appears finite & corrupt.

This will come to pass by an improvement of sensual enjoyment.

But first the notion that man has a body distinct from his soul is to be expunged; this I shall do, by printing in the infernal method, by corrosives, which in Hell are salutary and medicinal, melting apparent surfaces away, and displaying the infinite which was hid.

If the doors of perception were cleansed everything would appear to man as it is: infinite.

For man has closed himself up, till he sees all things thro' narrow chinks of his cavern.

A MEMORABLE FANCY

I was in a Printing house in Hell & saw the method in which knowledge is transmitted from generation to generation.

In the first chamber was a Dragon-Man, clearing away the rubbish from a cave's mouth; within, a number of Dragons were hollowing the cave.

In the second chamber was a Viper folding round the rock & the cave, and others adorning it with gold, silver, and precious stones.

In the third chamber was an Eagle with wings and feathers of air; he caused the inside of the cave to be infinite, around were numbers of Eaglelike men, who built palaces in the immense cliffs.

In the fourth chamber were Lions of flaming fire raging around & melting the metals into living fluids.

In the fifth chamber were Unnam'd forms, which cast the metals into the expanse.

There they were receiv'd by Men who occupied the sixth chamber, and took the forms of books & were arranged in libraries.

The Giants who formed this world into its sensual existence and now seem to live in it in chains, are in truth the causes of its life & the sources of all activity, but the chains are the cunning of weak and tame minds which have power to resist energy; according to the proverb, the weak in courage is strong in cunning.

Thus one portion of being is the Prolific; the other, the Devouring: to the devourer it seems as if the producer was in his chains, but it is not so, he only takes portions of existence and fancies that the whole.

But the Prolific would cease to be Prolific unless the Devourer as a sea received the excess of his delights.

Some will say, "Is not God alone the Prolific?" I answer, "God only Acts & Is, in existing beings or Men."

These two classes of men are always upon earth, & they should be enemies; whoever tries to reconcile them seeks to destroy existence.

Religion is an endeavor to reconcile the two.

Note. Jesus Christ did not wish to unite but to separate them, as in the Parable of sheep and goats! & he says, "I came not to send Peace but a Sword."

Messiah or Satan or Tempter was formerly thought to be one of the Antediluvians who are our Energies.

A Memorable Fancy

An Angel came to me and said, "O pitiable foolish young man! O horrible! O dreadful state! consider the hot burning dungeon thou art preparing for thyself to all eternity, to which thou art going in such career."

I said, "Perhaps you will be willing to show me my eternal lot & we will contemplate together upon it and see whether your lot or mine is most desirable."

So he took me thro' a stable & thro' a church & down into the church vault at the end of which was a mill: thro' the mill we went, and came to a cave; down the winding cavern we groped our tedious way till a void boundless as a nether sky appeared beneath us & we held by the roots of trees and hung over this immensity. But I said, "If you please we will commit ourselves to this void, and see whether Providence is here also; if you will not I will." But he answered, "Do not presume O young man, but as we here remain, behold thy lot which will soon appear when the darkness passes away."

So I remained with him sitting in the twisted root of an oak. He was suspended in a fungus which hung with the head downward into the deep.

By degrees we beheld the infinite Abyss, fiery as the smoke of a burning city; beneath us at an immense distance was the sun, black but shining; round it were fiery tracks on which revolv'd vast spiders, crawling after their prey; which flew or rather swum in the infinite deep, in the most terrific shapes of animals sprung from corruption; & the air was full of them, & seemed composed of them; these are Devils, and are called Powers of the air, I now asked my companion which was my eternal lot? He said, "Between the black & white spiders."

But now, from between the black & white spiders a cloud and fire burst and rolled thro' the deep, blackening all beneath, so that the nether deep grew black as a sea & rolled with a terrible noise; beneath us was nothing now to be seen but a black tempest, till looking east between the clouds & the waves, we saw a cataract of blood mixed with fire, and not many stones throw from us appeared and sunk again the scaly fold of a monstrous serpent. At last to the east, distant about three degrees, appeared a fiery crest above the waves. Slowly it reared like a ridge of golden rocks till we discovered two globes of crimson fire, from which the sea fled away in clouds of smoke, and now we saw it was the head of Leviathan; his forehead was divided into streaks of green & purple like those on a tyger's forehead: soon we saw his mouth & red gills hang just above the raging foam, tingeing the black deep with beams of blood, advancing toward us with all the fury of a spiritual existence.

My friend the Angel climb'd up from his station into the mill; I remain'd alone, & then this appearance was no more, but I found myself sitting on a pleasant bank beside a river by moonlight hearing a harper who sung to the harp, & his theme was, "The man who never alters his opinion is like standing water, & breeds reptiles of the mind."

But I arose, and sought for the mill, & there I found my Angel, who surprised asked me how I escaped?

I answered, "All that we saw was owing to your metaphysics: for when you ran away, I found myself on a bank by moonlight hearing a harper. But now we have seen my eternal lot, shall I show you yours?" He laughed at my proposal: but I by force suddenly caught him in my arms, & flew westerly thro' the night, till we were elevated above the earth's shadow: then I flung myself with him directly into the body of the sun; here I clothed myself in white, & taking in my hand Swedenborg's volumes sunk from the glorious clime, and passed all the planets till we came to Saturn; here I stayed to rest & then leap'd into the void, between Saturn & the fixed stars.

"Here," said I, "is your lot, in this space, if space it may be called." Soon we saw the stable and the church, & I took him to the altar and open'd the Bible, and lo! it was a deep pit, into which I descended, driving the Angel before me; soon we saw seven houses of brick, one we entered; in it were a number of monkeys, baboons, & all of that species, chained by the middle, grinning and snatching at one another, but withheld by the shortness of their chains: however I saw that they sometimes grew numerous, and then the weak were caught by the strong, and with a grinning aspect, first coupled with & then devoured, by plucking off first one limb and then another till the body was left a helpless trunk. This after grinning & kissing it with seeming fondness, they devoured too; and here & there I saw one savorily picking the flesh off of his own tail; as the stench terribly annoyed us both we went into the mill, & I in my hand brought the skeleton of a body, which in the mill was Aristotle's Analytics.

So the Angel said: "Thy fantasy has imposed upon me & thou oughtest to be ashamed."

I answered: "We impose on one another, & it is but lost time to converse with you whose works are only Analytics."

Opposition is true Friendship.

I have always found that Angels have the vanity to speak of themselves as the only wise; this they do with a confident insolence sprouting from systematic reasoning.

Thus Swedenborg boasts that what he writes is new; tho' it is only the Contents or Index of already publish'd books.

A man carried a monkey about for a show, & because he was a little wiser than the monkey, grew vain, and conceiv'd himself as much wiser than seven men. It is so with Swedenborg; he shows the folly of churches & exposes hypocrites, till he imagines that all are religious, & himself the single one on earth that ever broke a net.

Now hear a plain fact: Swedenborg has not written one new truth. Now hear another: he has written all the old falsehoods.

And now hear the reason. He conversed with Angels who are all religious, & conversed not with Devils, who all hate religion, for he was incapable thro' his conceited notions.

Thus Swedenborg's writings are a recapitulation of all superficial opinions, and an analysis of the more sublime, but no further.

Have now another plain fact: Any man of mechanical talents may from the writings of Paracelsus or Jacob Behmen, produce ten thousand volumes of equal value with Swedenborg's, and from those of Dante or Shakespeare, an infinite number.

But when he has done this, let him not say that he knows better than his master, for he only holds a candle in sunshine.

A Memorable Fancy

Once I saw a Devil in a flame of fire, who arose before an Angel that sat on a cloud, and the Devil uttered these words.

"The worship of God is: Honoring his gifts in other men each according to his genius, and loving the greatest men best: those who envy or calumniate great men hate God, for there is no other God."

The Angel hearing this became almost blue but mastering himself he grew yellow, & at last white, pink & smiling, and then replied:

"Thou Idolater, is not God One? & is not he visible in Jesus Christ? and has not Jesus Christ given his sanction to the law of ten commandments, and are not all other men fools, sinners, & nothings?"

The Devil answer'd, "Bray a fool in a mortar with wheat, yet shall not his folly be beaten out of him; if Jesus Christ is the greatest man, you ought to love him in the greatest degree; now hear how he has given his sanction to the law of ten commandments: did he not mock at the sabbath, and so mock the sabbath's God? murder those who were murdered because of him? turn away the law from the woman taken in adultery? steal the labor of others to support him? bear false witness when he omitted making a defense before Pilate? covet when he pray'd for his disciples, and when he bid them shake off the dust of their feet against such as refused to lodge them? I tell you, no virtue can exist without breaking these ten commandments. Jesus was all virtue, and acted from impulse, not from rules."

When he had so spoken, I beheld the Angel, who stretched out his arms, embracing the flame of fire & he was consumed and arose as Elijah.

Note. This Angel, who is now become a Devil, is my particular friend; we often read the Bible together in its infernal or diabolical sense, which the world shall have if they behave well.

I have also The Bible of Hell, which the world shall have whether they will or no.

One Law for the Lion & Ox is Oppression.

A SONG OF LIBERTY

1. The Eternal Female groaned! it was heard over all the Earth.

2. Albion's coast is sick, silent; the American meadows faint!

3. Shadows of Prophecy shiver along by the lakes and the rivers and mutter across the ocean! France rend down thy dungeon!

4. Golden Spain, burst the barriers of old Rome!

5. Cast thy keys O Rome into the deep down falling, even to eternity down falling,

6. And weep!

7. In her trembling hands she took the newborn terror howling;

8. On those infinite mountains of light now barr'd out by the Atlantic sea, the newborn fire stood before the starry king!

9. Flagg'd with gray brow'd snows and thunderous visages the jealous wings wav'd over the deep.

10. The speary hand burned aloft, unbuckled was the shield, forth went the hand of jealousy among the flaming hair, and hurl'd the newborn wonder thro' the starry night.

11. The fire, the fire, is falling!

12. Look up! look up! O citizen of London, enlarge thy countenance! O Jew, leave counting gold! return to thy oil and wine. O African! black African! (go wingéd thought, widen his forehead.)

13. The fiery limbs, the flaming hair, shot like the sinking sun into the western sea.

14. Wak'd from his eternal sleep, the hoary element roaring fled away:

15. Down rushed, beating his wings in vain, the jealous king; his gray-brow'd counsellors, thunderous warriors, curl'd

veterans, among helms, and shields, and chariots, horses, elephants, banners, castles, slings and rocks,

16. Falling, rushing, ruining! buried in the ruins, on Urthona's dens.

17. All night beneath the ruins, then their sullen flames faded emerge round the gloomy king,

18. With thunder and fire, leading his starry hosts thro' the waste wilderness he promulgates his ten commands, glancing his beamy eyelids over the deep in dark dismay,

19. Where the son of fire in his eastern cloud, while the morning plumes her golden breast,

20. Spurning the clouds written with curses, stamps the stony law to dust, loosing the eternal horses from the dens of night, crying: "Empire is no more! and now the lion & wolf shall cease."

Chorus

Let the Priests of the Raven of dawn, no longer in deadly black, with hoarse note curse the sons of joy. Nor his accepted brethren whom, tyrant, he calls free, lay the bound or build the roof. Nor pale religious lechery call that virginity, that wishes but acts not!

For everything that lives is Holy.

America:
A Prophecy

AMERICA: A PROPHECY

PRELUDIUM

The shadowy Daughter of Urthona stood before red Orc,
When fourteen suns had faintly journey'd o'er his dark abode:
His food she brought in iron baskets, his drink in cups of iron:
Crown'd with a helmet & dark hair the nameless female stood;
A quiver with its burning stores, a bow like that of night,
When pestilence is shot from heaven: no other arms she need!
Invulnerable tho' naked, save where clouds roll round her
    loins
Their awful folds in the dark air: silent she stood as night;
For never from her iron tongue could voice or sound arise,
But dumb till that dread day when Orc assay'd his fierce
    embrace.

"Dark Virgin," said the hairy youth, "thy father stern, abhorr'd,
Rivets my tenfold chains while still on high my spirit soars;
Sometimes an eagle screaming in the sky, sometimes a lion
Stalking upon the mountains, & sometimes a whale, I lash
The raging fathomless abyss; anon a serpent folding
Around the pillars of Urthona, and round thy dark limbs
On the Canadian wilds I fold; feeble my spirit folds,
For chain'd beneath I rend these caverns: when thou bringest
    food
I howl my joy, and my red eyes seek to behold thy face—
In vain! these clouds roll to & fro, & hide thee from my
    sight."

Silent as despairing love, and strong as jealousy,
The hairy shoulders rend the links; free are the wrists of fire;
Round the terrific loins he seiz'd the panting, struggling womb;
It joy'd: she put aside her clouds & smiled her firstborn smile,
As when a black cloud shows its lightnings to the silent deep.

Soon as she saw the terrible boy, then burst the virgin cry:

"I know thee, I have found thee, & I will not let thee go:
Thou art the image of God who dwells in darkness of Africa,
And thou art fall'n to give me life in regions of dark death.
On my American plains I feel the struggling afflictions
Endur'd by roots that writhe their arms into the nether deep.
I see a Serpent in Canada who courts me to his love,
In Mexico an Eagle, and a Lion in Peru;
I see a Whale in the South Sea, drinking my soul away.
O what limb rending pains I feel! thy fire & my frost
Mingle in howling pains, in furrows by thy lightnings rent.
This is eternal death, and this the torment long foretold."

A Prophecy

The Guardian Prince of Albion burns in his nightly tent:
Sullen fires across the Atlantic glow to America's shore,
Piercing the souls of warlike men who rise in silent night.
Washington, Franklin, Paine & Warren, Gates, Hancock &
    Green
Meet on the coast glowing with blood from Albion's fiery
    Prince.

Washington spoke: "Friends of America! Look over the
    Atlantic sea;
A bended bow is lifted in heaven, & a heavy iron chain
Descends, link by link, from Albion's cliffs across the sea, to
    bind
Brothers & sons of America till our faces pale and yellow,
Heads depressed, voices weak, eyes downcast, hands
    work-bruis'd,
Feet bleeding on the sultry sands, and the furrows of the
    whip
Descend to generations that in future times forget."

The strong voice ceas'd, for a terrible blast swept over the
 heaving sea:
The eastern cloud rent: on his cliffs stood Albion's wrathful
 Prince,
A dragon form, clashing his scales: at midnight he arose,
And flam'd red meteors round the land of Albion beneath;
His voice, his locks, his awful shoulders, and his glowing eyes
Appear to the Americans upon the cloudy night.
Solemn heave the Atlantic waves between the gloomy nations,
Swelling, belching from its deeps red clouds & raging fires.
Albion is sick! America faints! enrag'd the Zenith grew.
As human blood shooting its veins all round the orbed heaven,
Red rose the clouds from the Atlantic in vast wheels of blood,
And in the red clouds rose a Wonder o'er the Atlantic sea,
Intense! naked! a Human fire, fierce glowing, as the wedge
Of iron heated in the furnace: his terrible limbs were fire
With myriads of cloudy terrors, banners dark & towers
Surrounded: heat but not light went thro' the murky
 atmosphere.

The King of England looking westward trembles at the vision.

Albion's Angel stood beside the stone of night, and saw
The terror like a comet, or more like the planet red
That once enclos'd the terrible wandering comets in its
 sphere.
Then, Mars, thou wast our center, & the planets three flew
 round
Thy crimson disk: so e'er the Sun was rent from thy red
 sphere.
The Specter glow'd his horrid length staining the temple long
With beams of blood; & thus a voice came forth, and shook
 the temple:

"The morning comes, the night decays, the watchmen leave
 their stations;
The grave is burst, the spices shed, the linen wrapped up;

The bones of death, the cov'ring clay, the sinews shrunk &
    dried
Reviving shake, inspiring move, breathing, awakening,
Spring like redeemed captives when their bonds & bars are
    burst.
Let the slave grinding at the mill run out into the field,
Let him look up into the heavens & laugh in the bright air,
Let the enchained soul, shut up in darkness and in sighing,
Whose face has never seen a smile in thirty weary years,
Rise and look out; his chains are loose, his dungeon doors are
    open;
And let his wife and children return from the oppressor's
    scourge.
They look behind at every step & believe it is a dream,
Singing: "The Sun has left his blackness & has found a fresher
    morning,
And the fair Moon rejoices in the clear & cloudless night;
For Empire is no more, and now the Lion & Wolf shall
    cease."

In thunders ends the voice. Then Albion's Angel wrathful
    burnt
Beside the Stone of Night, and like the Eternal Lion's howl
In famine & war, replied: "Art thou not Orc, who
    serpent-form'd
Stands at the gate of Enitharmon to devour her children?
Blasphemous Demon, Antichrist, hater of Dignities,
Lover of wild rebellion, and transgressor of God's Law,
Why dost thou come to Angel's eyes in this terrific form?"

The Terror answer'd: "I am Orc, wreath'd round the accursed
    tree:
The times are ended; shadows pass, the morning 'gins to break;
The fiery joy, that Urizen perverted to ten commands,
What night he led the starry hosts thro' the wide wilderness,
That stony law I stamp to dust; and scatter religion abroad

To the four winds as a torn book, & none shall gather the
    leaves;
But they shall rot on desert sands, & consume in bottomless
    deeps,
To make the deserts blossom, & the deeps shrink to their
    fountains,
And to renew the fiery joy, and burst the stony roof;
That pale religious lechery, seeking Virginity,
May find it in a harlot, and in coarse-clad honesty
The undefil'd, tho' ravish'd in her cradle night and morn;
For everything that lives is holy, life delights in life;
Because the soul of sweet delight can never be defil'd.
Fires enwrap the earthly globe, yet man is not consum'd;
Amidst the lustful fires he walks; his feet become like
    brass,
His knees and thighs like silver, & his breast and head like
    gold."

"Sound! sound! my loud war-trumpets, & alarm my Thirteen
    Angels!
Loud howls the eternal Wolf! the eternal Lion lashes his tail!
America is darken'd; and my punishing Demons, terrified,
Crouch howling before their caverns deep, like skins dried in
    the wind.
They cannot smite the wheat, nor quench the fatness of the
    earth;
They cannot smite with sorrows, nor subdue the plow and
    spade;
They cannot wall the city, nor moat round the castle of princes;
They cannot bring the stubbed oak to overgrow the hills;
For terrible men stand on the shores, & in their robes I see
Children take shelter from the lightnings: there stands
    Washington
And Paine and Warren with their foreheads rear'd toward the
    east.
But clouds obscure my aged sight. A vision from afar!

Sound! sound! my loud war-trumpets, & alarm my thirteen
    Angels!
Ah vision from afar! Ah rebel form that rent the ancient
Heavens! Eternal Viper, self-renew'd, rolling in clouds,
I see thee in thick clouds and darkness on America's shore,
Writhing in pangs of abhorred birth; red flames the crest
    rebellious
And eyes of death; the harlot womb, oft opened in vain,
Heaves in enormous circles: now the times are return'd upon
    thee,
Devourer of thy parent, now thy unutterable torment renews.
Sound! sound! my loud war-trumpets, & alarm my thirteen
    Angels!
Ah terrible birth! a young one bursting! where is the weeping
    mouth,
And where the mother's milk? instead, those ever-hissing jaws
And parched lips drop with fresh gore: now roll thou in the
    clouds;
Thy mother lays her length outstretch'd upon the shore
    beneath.
Sound! sound! my loud war-trumpets, & alarm my thirteen
    Angels!
Loud howls the eternal Wolf! the eternal Lion lashes his tail!"

Thus wept the Angel voice, & as he wept, the terrible blasts
Of trumpets blew a loud alarm across the Atlantic deep.
No trumpets answer; no reply of clarions or of fifes:
Silent the Colonies remain and refuse the loud alarm.

On those vast shady hills between America & Albion's shore,
Now barr'd out by the Atlantic sea, called Atlantean hills,
Because from their bright summits you may pass to the
    Golden world,
An ancient palace, archetype of mighty Emperies,
Rears its immortal pinnacles, built in the forest of God
By Ariston, the king of beauty, for his stolen bride.

Here on their magic seats the thirteen Angels sat perturb'd,
For clouds from the Atlantic hover o'er the solemn roof.

Fiery the Angels rose, & as they rose deep thunder rolled
Around their shores, indignant burning with the fires of Orc;
And Boston's angel cried aloud as they flew thro' the dark
    night.

He cried: "Why trembles honesty, and like a murderer
Why seeks he refuge from the frowns of his immortal station?
Must the generous tremble & leave his joy to the idle, to the
    pestilence,
That mock him? who commanded this? what God? what
    Angel?
To keep the gen'rous from experience till the ungenerous
Are unrestrain'd performers of the energies of nature;
Till pity is become a trade, and generosity a science
That men get rich by; & the sandy desert is giv'n to the strong?
What God is he writes laws of peace & clothes him in a
    tempest?
What pitying Angel lusts for tears and fans himself with sighs?
What crawling villain preaches abstinence & wraps himself
In fat of lambs? no more I follow, no more obedience pay!"

So cried he, rending off his robe & throwing down his
    scepter
In sight of Albion's Guardian; and all the thirteen Angels
Rent off their robes to the hungry wind, & threw their golden
    scepters
Down on the land of America; indignant they descended
Headlong from out their heav'nly heights, descending swift as
    fires
Over the land; naked & flaming are their lineaments seen
In the deep gloom; by Washington & Paine & Warren they
    stood;
And the flame folded, roaring fierce within the pitchy night

Before the Demon red, who burnt towards America,
In black smoke, thunders, and loud winds, rejoicing in its
    terror,
Breaking in smoky wreaths from the wild deep, & gath'ring
    thick
In flames as of a furnace on the land from North to South,
What time the thirteen Governors that England sent, convene
In Bernard's house; the flames cover'd the land, they rouse,
    they cry;
Shaking their mental chains, they rush in fury to the sea
To quench their anguish; at the feet of Washington downfall'n
They grovel on the sand and writhing lie, while all
The British soldiers thro' the thirteen states sent up a howl
Of anguish, threw their swords & muskets to the earth, & ran
From their encampments and dark castles, seeking where to
    hide
From the grim flames, and from the visions of Orc, in sight
Of Albion's Angel; who, enrag'd, his secret clouds open'd
From north to south and burnt outstretch'd on wings of wrath,
    cov'ring
The eastern sky, spreading his awful wings across the heavens.
Beneath him rolled his num'rous hosts, all Albion's Angels
    camp'd
Darken'd the Atlantic mountains; & their trumpets shook the
    valleys,
Arm'd with diseases of the earth to cast upon the Abyss,
Their numbers forty millions, must'ring in the eastern sky.

In the flames stood & view'd the armies drawn out in the sky,
Washington, Franklin, Paine, & Warren, Allen, Gates, & Lee,
And heard the voice of Albion's Angel give the thunderous
    command;
His plagues, obedient to his voice, flew forth out of their
    clouds,
Falling upon America, as a storm to cut them off,
As a blight cuts the tender corn when it begins to appear.

Dark is the heaven above, & cold & hard the earth beneath:
And as a plague wind fill'd with insects cuts off man & beast,
And as a sea o'erwhelms a land in the day of an earthquake,
Fury! rage! madness! in a wind swept through America;
And the red flames of Orc, that folded roaring, fierce, around
The angry shores; and the fierce rushing of th' inhabitants
    together!
The citizens of New York close their books & lock their chests;
The mariners of Boston drop their anchors and unlade;
The scribe of Pennsylvania casts his pen upon the earth;
The builder of Virginia throws his hammer down in fear.

Then had America been lost, o'erwhelm'd by the Atlantic,
And Earth had lost another portion of the infinite,
But all rush together in the night in wrath and raging fire.
The red fires rag'd! the plagues recoil'd! then rolled they back
    with fury
On Albion's Angels: then the Pestilence began in streaks of
    red
Across the limbs of Albion's Guardian; the spotted plague
    smote Bristol's
And the Leprosy London's Spirit, sickening all their bands:
The millions sent up a howl of anguish and threw off their
    hammer'd mail,
And cast their swords & spears to earth, & stood, a naked
    multitude:
Albion's Guardian writhed in torment on the eastern sky,
Pale, quiv'ring toward the brain his glimmering eyes, teeth
    chattering.
Howling & shuddering, his legs quivering, convuls'd each
    muscle & sinew:
Sick'ning lay London's Guardian, and the ancient mitered
    York,
Their heads on snowy hills, their ensigns sick'ning in the sky.
The plagues creep on the burning winds driven by flames of
    Orc,

And by the fierce Americans rushing together in the night,
Driven o'er the Guardians of Ireland, and Scotland and Wales.
They, spotted with plagues, forsook the frontiers; & their
    banners, sear'd
With fires of hell, deform their ancient heavens with shame
    & woe.
Hid in his caves the Bard of Albion felt the enormous plagues,
And a cowl of flesh grew o'er his head, & scales on his back
    & ribs;
And, rough with black scales, all his Angels fright their ancient
    heavens.
The doors of marriage are open, and the Priests in rustling
    scales
Rush into reptile coverts, hiding from the fires of Orc,
That play around the golden roofs in wreaths of fierce desire,
Leaving the females naked and glowing with the lusts of youth.
For the female spirits of the dead, pining in bonds of religion,
Run from their fetters reddening, & in long drawn arches
    sitting,
They feel the nerves of youth renew, and desires of ancient
    times
Over their pale limbs, as a vine when the tender grape appears.

Over the hills, the vales, the cities, rage the red flames fierce:
The Heavens melted from north to south; and Urizen, who sat
Above all heavens, in thunders wrapp'd, emerg'd his leprous
    head
From out his holy shrine, his tears in deluge piteous
Falling into the deep sublime; flagg'd with gray-brow'd snows
And thunderous visages, his jealous wings wav'd over the deep;
Weeping in dismal howling woe, he dark descended, howling
Around the smitten bands, clothed in tears & trembling,
    shudd'ring cold.
His stored snows he poured forth, and his icy magazines
He open'd on the deep, and on the Atlantic sea white shiv'ring
Leprous his limbs, all over white, and hoary was his visage,
Weeping in dismal howlings before the stern Americans,

Hiding the Demon red with clouds & cold mists from the
    earth;
Till Angels & weak men twelve years should govern o'er the
    strong;
And then their end should come, when France receiv'd the
    Demon's light.

Stiff shudderings shook the heav'nly thrones! France, Spain,
    & Italy
In terror view'd the bands of Albion, and the ancient
    Guardians,
Fainting upon the elements, smitten with their own plagues.
They slow advance to shut the five gates of their law-built
    heaven,
Filled with blasting fancies and with mildews of despair,
With fierce disease and lust, unable to stem the fires of Orc.
But the five gates were consum'd, & their bolts and hinges
    melted;
And the fierce flames burnt round the heavens & round the
    abodes of men.

FINIS

[CANCELLED PLATES]

The Guardian Prince of Albion burns in his nightly tent:
Sullen fires across the Atlantic glow to America's shore,
Piercing the souls of warlike men who rise in silent night.
Washington, Hancock, Paine & Warren, Gates, Franklin &
    Green
Meet on the coast glowing with blood from Albion's fiery
    Prince.
Washington spoke: "Friends of America! look over the Atlantic
    sea;
A bended bow in heaven is lifted, & a heavy iron chain
Descends, link by link, from Albion's cliffs across the sea, to
    bind

Brothers & sons of America till our faces pale and yellow,
Heads depressed, voices weak, eyes downcast, hands work-
    bruised,
Feet bleeding on the sultry sands, & the furrows of the whip
Descend to generations that in future times forget."
The strong voice ceas'd, for a terrible blast swept over the
    heaving sea:
The eastern cloud rent: on his cliffs stood Albion's fiery Prince,
A dragon form, clashing his scales: at midnight he arose,
And flam'd fierce meteors round the band of Albion beneath;
His voice, his locks, his awful shoulders, & his glowing eyes
Reveal the dragon thro' the human; coursing swift as fire
To the close hall of counsel, where his Angel form renews.
In a sweet vale shelter'd with cedars, that eternal stretch
Their unmov'd branches, stood the hall, built when the moon
    shot forth,
In that dread night when Urizen call'd the stars round his feet;
Then burst the center from its orb, and found a place beneath;
And Earth conglob'd, in narrow room, rolled round its sulphur
    Sun.
To this deep valley situated by the flowing Thames,
Where George the third holds council & his Lords &
    Commons meet,
Shut out from mortal sight the Angel came; the vale was dark
With clouds of smoke from the Atlantic, that in volumes rolled
Between the mountains; dismal visions mope around the house
On chairs of iron, canopied with mystic ornaments
Of life by magic power condens'd; infernal forms art-bound
The council sat; all rose before the aged apparition,
His snowy beard that streams like lambent flames down his
    wide breast
Wetting with tears, & his white garments cast a wintry light.
Then as arm'd clouds arise terrific round the northern drum,
The world is silent at the flapping of the folding banners.
So still terrors rent the house, as when the solemn globe
Launch'd to the unknown shore, while Sotha held the
    northern helm,

Till to that void it came & fell; so the dark house was rent.
The valley mov'd beneath; its shining pillars split in twain,
And its roofs crack across down falling on th' Angelic seats.

Then Albion's Angel rose resolv'd to the cove of armory:
His shield that bound twelve demons & their cities in its orb
He took down from its trembling pillar; from its cavern deep,
His helm was brought by London's Guardian, & his thirsty
    spear
By the wise spirit of London's river; silent stood the King
    breathing damp mists,
And on his aged limbs they clasp'd the armor of terrible gold.
Infinite London's awful spires cast a dreadful cold
Even on rational things beneath and from the palace walls
Around Saint James's, chill & heavy, even to the city gate.
On the vast stone whose name is Truth he stood, his cloudy
    shield
Smote with his scepter, the scale bound orb loud howl'd; the
    pillar
Trembling sunk, an earthquake rolled along the mossy pile.
In glitt'ring armor, swift as winds, intelligent as clouds
Four winged heralds mount the furious blasts & blow their
    trumps;
Gold, silver, brass & iron clangors clamoring rend the shores.
Like white clouds rising from the deeps his fifty-two armies
From the four cliffs of Albion rise, mustering around their
    Prince;
Angels of cities and of parishes and villages and families,
In armor as the nerves of wisdom, each his station holds.
In opposition dire, a warlike cloud, the myriads stood
In the red air before the Demon seen even by mortal men,
Who call it Fancy, or shut the gates of sense, or in their
    chambers
Sleep like the dead. But like a constellation ris'n and blazing
Over the rugged ocean, so the Angels of Albion hung
Over the frowning shadow like an aged King in arms of gold,

Who wept over a den, in which his only son outstretch'd
By rebels' hands was slain; his white beard wav'd in the wild
    wind.
On mountains & cliffs of snow the awful apparition hover'd,
And like the voices of religious dead heard in the mountains
When holy zeal scents the sweet valleys of ripe virgin bliss,
Such was the hollow voice that o'er America lamented.

Europe:
A Prophecy

EUROPE: A PROPHECY

[INTRODUCTION]

"Five windows light the cavern'd Man: thro' one he breathes
    the air;
Thro' one hears music of the spheres; thro' one the eternal
    vine
Flourishes, that he may receive the grapes; thro' one can look
And see small portions of the eternal world that ever groweth;
Thro' one himself pass out what time he please; but he will
    not,
For stolen joys are sweet & bread eaten in secret pleasant."

So sang a Fairy, mocking, as he sat on a streak'd Tulip,
Thinking none saw him: when he ceas'd I started from the
    trees
And caught him in my hat, as boys knock down a butterfly.
"How know you this," said I, "small Sir? where did you learn
    this song?"
Seeing himself in my possession, thus he answer'd me:
"My master, I am yours! command me, for I must obey."

"Then tell me, what is the material world, and is it dead?"
He, laughing, answer'd: "I will write a book on leaves of
    flowers,
If you will feed me on love-thoughts & give me now and then
A cup of sparkling poetic fancies; so, when I am tipsy,
I'll sing to you to this soft lute, and show you all alive
The world, where every particle of dust breathes forth its joy."

I took him home in my warm bosom: as we went along
Wildflowers I gather'd, & he show'd me each eternal flower:

He laugh'd aloud to see them whimper because they were
    pluck'd.
They hover'd round me like a cloud of incense: when I came
Into my parlor and sat down and took my pen to write,
My Fairy sat upon the table and dictated EUROPE.

PRELUDIUM

The nameless shadowy female rose from out the breast of
    Orc,
Her snaky hair brandishing in the winds of Enitharmon;
And thus her voice arose:

"O mother Enitharmon, wilt thou bring forth other sons?
To cause my name to vanish, that my place may not be found,
For I am faint with travail,
Like the dark cloud disburden'd in the day of dismal thunder.

"My roots are brandish'd in the heavens, my fruits in earth
    beneath
Surge, foam and labor into life, firstborn & first consum'd!
Consumed and consuming!
Then why shouldst thou, accursed mother, bring me into life?

"I wrap my turban of thick clouds around my lab'ring head,
And fold the sheety waters as a mantle round my limbs;
Yet the red sun and moon
And all the overflowing stars rain down prolific pains.

"Unwilling I look up to heaven, unwilling count the stars:
Sitting in fathomless abyss of my immortal shrine
I seize their burning power
And bring forth howling terrors, all devouring fiery kings,

"Devouring & devoured, roaming on dark and desolate
    mountains,
In forests of eternal death, shrieking in hollow trees.

Ah mother Enitharmon!
Stamp not with solid form this vig'rous progeny of fires.
"I bring forth from my teeming bosom myriads of flames,
And thou dost stamp them with a signet; then they roam
    abroad
And leave me void as death.
Ah! I am drown'd in shady woe and visionary joy.

"And who shall bind the infinite with an eternal band?
To compass it with swaddling bands? and who shall cherish it
With milk and honey?
I see it smile, & I roll inward, & my voice is past."

        She ceased, & rolled her shady clouds
        Into the secret place.

A Prophecy

  The deep of winter came,
  What time the secret child
  Descended thro' the orient gates of the eternal day:
  War ceas'd, & all the troops like shadows fled to their abodes.

  Then Enitharmon saw her sons & daughters rise around;
  Like pearly clouds they meet together in the crystal house;
  And Los, possessor of the moon, joy'd in the peaceful night,
  Thus speaking, while his num'rous sons shook their bright
      fiery wings:

  "Again the night is come
  That strong Urthona takes his rest;
  And Urizen, unloos'd from chains,
  Glows like a meteor in the distant north.
  Stretch forth your hands and strike the elemental strings!
  Awake the thunders of the deep!
  The shrill winds wake,

Till all the sons of Urizen look out and envy Los.
Seize all the spirits of life, and bind
Their warbling joys to our loud strings!
Bind all the nourishing sweets of earth
To give us bliss, that we may drink the sparkling wine of Los!
And let us laugh at war,
Despising toil and care,
Because the days and nights of joy in lucky hours renew.

"Arise, O Orc, from thy deep den!
Firstborn of Enitharmon, rise!
And we will crown thy head with garlands of the ruddy vine;
For now thou art bound,
And I may see thee in the hour of bliss, my eldest born."

The horrent Demon rose surrounded with red stars of fire
Whirling about in furious circles round the immortal fiend.

Then Enitharmon down descended into his red light,
And thus her voice rose to her children: the distant heavens
        reply:

"Now comes the night of Enitharmon's joy!
Who shall I call? Who shall I send,
That Woman, lovely Woman, may have dominion?
Arise, O Rintrah, thee I call! & Palamabron, thee!
Go! tell the Human race that Woman's love is Sin;
That an Eternal life awaits the worms of sixty winters
In an allegorical abode where existence hath never come.
Forbid all Joy, & from her childhood shall the little female
Spread nets in every secret path.

"My weary eyelids draw towards the evening; my bliss is yet
        but new.

"Arise, O Rintrah, eldest born, second to none but Orc!
O lion Rintrah, raise thy fury from thy forests black!

Bring Palamabron, horned priest, skipping upon the mountains,
And silent Elynittria, the silver bowed queen.
Rintrah, where hast thou hid thy bride?
Weeps she in desert shades?
Alas! my Rintrah, bring the lovely jealous Ocalythron.

"Arise, my son! bring all thy brethren, O thou king of fire!
Prince of the sun! I see thee with thy innumerable race,
Thick as the summer stars;
But each, ramping, his golden mane shakes,
And thine eyes rejoice because of strength, O Rintrah, furious
    king!"

Enitharmon slept
Eighteen hundred years. Man was a Dream!
The night of Nature and their harps unstrung!
She slept in middle of her nightly song
Eighteen hundred years, a female dream.

Shadows of men in fleeting bands upon the winds
Divide the heavens of Europe
Till Albion's Angel, smitten with his own plagues, fled with his
    bands.
The cloud bears hard on Albion's shore,
Fill'd with immortal demons of futurity:
In council gather the smitten Angels of Albion;
The cloud bears hard upon the council house, down rushing
On the heads of Albion's Angels.

One hour they lay buried beneath the ruins of that hall;
But as the stars rise from the salt lake, they arise in pain,
In troubled mists, o'erclouded by the terrors of struggling
    times.

In thoughts perturb'd they rose from the bright ruins, silent
    following
The fiery King, who sought his ancient temple, serpent-form'd,

That stretches out its shady length along the Island white.
Round him rolled his clouds of war; silent the Angel went
Along the infinite shores of Thames to golden Verulam.
There stand the venerable porches that high-towering rear
Their oak-surrounded pillars, form'd of massy stones, uncut
With tool, stones precious, such eternal in the heavens,
Of colors twelve, few known on earth, give light in the opaque,
Plac'd in the order of the stars, when the five senses whelm'd
In deluge o'er the earthborn man; then turn'd the fluxile eyes
Into two stationary orbs, concentrating all things:
The ever-varying spiral ascents to the heavens of heavens
Were bended downward, and the nostrils' golden gates shut,
Turn'd outward, barr'd and petrified against the infinite.

Thought chang'd the infinite to a serpent, that which pitieth
To a devouring flame; and man fled from its face and hid
In forests of night: then all the eternal forests were divided
Into earths rolling in circles of space, that like an ocean rush'd
And overwhelmed all except this finite wall of flesh.
Then was the serpent temple form'd, image of infinite
Shut up in finite revolutions, and man became an Angel,
Heaven a mighty circle turning, God a tyrant crown'd.

Now arriv'd the ancient Guardian at the southern porch
That planted thick with trees of blackest leaf & in a vale
Obscure enclos'd the Stone of Night; oblique it stood, o'erhung
With purple flowers and berries red, image of that sweet south
Once open to the heavens, and elevated on the human neck,
Now overgrown with hair and cover'd with a stony roof.
Downward 'tis sunk beneath th' attractive north, that round
      the feet,
A raging whirlpool, draws the dizzy enquirer to his grave.

      Albion's Angel rose upon the Stone of Night.
      He saw Urizen on the Atlantic;
      And his brazen Book
      That Kings & Priests had copied on Earth,
      Expanded from North to South.

And the clouds & fires pale rolled round in the night of
Enitharmon,
Round Albion's cliffs & London's walls: still Enitharmon
slept.
Rolling volumes of gray mist involve Churches, Palaces,
Towers;
For Urizen unclasp'd his Book, feeding his soul with pity.
The youth of England, hid in gloom, curse the pain'd
heavens, compell'd
Into the deadly night to see the form of Albion's Angel.
Their parents brought them forth, & aged ignorance
preaches, canting,
On a vast rock, perceiv'd by those senses that are clos'd
from thought:
Bleak, dark, abrupt it stands & overshadows London city.
They saw his boney feet on the rock, the flesh consum'd
in flames;
They saw the Serpent temple lifted above, shadowing
the Island white;
They heard the voice of Albion's Angel howling in flames
of Orc,
Seeking the trump of the last doom.

Above the rest the howl was heard from Westminster
louder & louder:
The Guardian of the secret codes forsook his ancient
mansion,
Driven out by the flames of Orc; his furr'd robes & false
locks
Adhered and grew one with his flesh, and nerves & veins
shot thro' them.
With dismal torment sick, hanging upon the wind, he fled
Groveling along Great George Street thro' the Park gate:
all the soldiers
Fled from his sight: he dragg'd his torments to the wilderness.

Thus was the howl thro' Europe!
For Orc rejoic'd to hear the howling shadows;

But Palamabron shot his lightnings, trenching down his wide
    back;
And Rintrah hung with all his legions in the nether deep.

Enitharmon laugh'd in her sleep to see (O woman's triumph!)
Every house a den, every man bound: the shadows are fill'd
With specters, and the windows wove over with curses of iron:
Over the doors "Thou shalt not," & over the chimneys
    "Fear" is written:
With bands of iron round their necks fasten'd into the walls
The citizens, in leaden gyves the inhabitants of suburbs
Walk heavy; soft and bent are the bones of villagers.

Between the clouds of Urizen the flames of Orc roll heavy
Around the limbs of Albion's Guardian, his flesh consuming:
Howlings & hissings, shrieks & groans, & voices of despair
Arise around him in the cloudy heavens of Albion. Furious,
The red limb'd Angel seiz'd in horror and torment
The Trump of the last doom; but he could not blow the iron
    tube!
Thrice he assay'd presumptuous to awake the dead to
    Judgment.

A mighty Spirit leap'd from the land of Albion,
Nam'd Newton: he seiz'd the trump & blow'd the enormous
    blast!
Yellow as leaves of Autumn, the myriads of Angelic hosts
Fell thro' the wintry skies seeking their graves,
Rattling their hollow bones in howling and lamentation.

Then Enitharmon woke, nor knew that she had slept;
And eighteen hundred years were fled
As if they had not been.
She call'd her sons & daughters
To the sports of night
Within her crystal house,
And thus her song proceeds:

"Arise, Ethinthus! tho' the earthworm call,
Let him call in vain,
Till the night of holy shadows
And human solitude is past!

"Ethinthus, queen of waters, how thou shinest in the sky!
My daughter, how do I rejoice! for thy children flock around
Like the gay fishes on the wave, when the cold moon drinks
    the dew.
Ethinthus! thou art sweet as comforts to my fainting soul,
For now thy waters warble round the feet of Enitharmon.

"Manathu-Varcyon! I behold thee flaming in my halls,
Light of thy mother's soul! I see thy lovely eagles round;
Thy golden wings are my delight, & thy flames of soft delusion.

"Where is my luring bird of Eden? Leutha, silent love!
Leutha, the many color'd bow delights upon thy wings:
Soft soul of flowers, Leutha!
Sweet smiling pestilence! I see thy blushing light;
Thy daughters, many changing,
Revolve like sweet perfumes ascending, O Leutha, silken
    queen!

"Where is the youthful Antamon, prince of the pearly dew?
O Antamon! why wilt thou leave thy mother Enitharmon?
Alone I see thee, crystal form,
Floating upon the bosom'd air
With lineaments of gratified desire.
My Antamon, the seven churches of Leutha seek thy love.

"I hear the soft Oothoon in Enitharmon's tents;
Why wilt thou give up woman's secrecy, my melancholy child?
Between two moments bliss is ripe.
O Theotormon! robb'd of joy, I see thy salt tears flow
Down the steps of my crystal house.

"Sotha & Thiralatha! secret dwellers of dreamful caves,
Arise and please the horrent fiend with your melodious songs;
Still all your thunders, golden-hoof'd, & bind your horses
    black.
Orc! smile upon my children!
Smile, son of my afflictions.
Arise, O Orc, and give our mountains joy of thy red light!"

She ceas'd; for All were forth at sport beneath the solemn
    moon
Waking the stars of Urizen with their immortal songs,
That nature felt thro' all her pores the enormous revelry
Till morning oped the eastern gate;
Then everyone fled to his station, & Enitharmon wept.

But terrible Orc, when he beheld the morning in the east,
Shot from the heights of Enitharmon,
And in the vineyards of red France appear'd the light of his
    fury.

The sun glow'd fiery red!
The furious terrors flew around
On golden chariots raging with red wheels dropping with
    blood!
The Lions lash their wrathful tails!
The Tigers couch upon the prey & suck the ruddy tide,
And Enitharmon groans & cries in anguish and dismay.

Then Los arose: his head he rear'd in snaky thunders clad;
And with a cry that shook all nature to the utmost pole,
Call'd all his sons to the strife of blood.

FINIS

INDEX OF TITLES AND FIRST LINES